THIRTY MINUTES
FOR GOD

André Sève, A.A.

THIRTY MINUTES
FOR GOD

New City Press

Published in the United States by New City Press
the Publishing House of the Focolare
206 Skillman Avenue, Brooklyn, NY 11211
©1986 by New City Press, New York

Translated by M. Angeline Bouchard
from the original French edition
Trente Minutes Pour Dieu

Cover design by Nick Cianfarani
Library of Congress Catalog Number: 85-072398
ISBN 0-911782-49-4
Printed in the United States of America

Nihil Obstat: Reverend John Brown S.T.L., Delegated Censor
Imprimatur: Francis J. Mugavero, D.D., Bishop of Brooklyn
Brooklyn, N.Y., May 21, 1986

TABLE OF CONTENTS

Thirty Minutes for God   7

Of What Use is Prayer, Anyway?   13

A Boundless Trust in God   19

"Make Me Want to Pray"   25

The Spirit is Always Given to Those who Pray . .   31

Our Daily Life is the Most Sacred of All   37

Am I Madly in Love with God?   43

Let Us Place Ourselves in God's Presence   49

God Will Act   59

Being with God All Day?   67

Are We to Pray or Build Up the World   73

Broad Horizons   79

Pray to Keep Up with the Current   87

Pray to Keep Going Against the Current   93

A Comfortable Armchair, Cold Beer, and TV . . .   99

Wake Up!   105

We are Always Rejoicing (?)   111

The Spiritual Realism of Thérèse of Lisieux   119

For years I meditated daily. Little by little, I gave it up. Then one day I was sent to a "House of Prayer" as a reporter. I went along with what the others were doing. On the first morning, we had 30 minutes of meditation, called "mental prayer"—30 minutes of such spiritual dryness that I was forced to tell myself: "Since you gave up meditation, it's funny how you drifted far from . . . ."

Far from what? From God? But when someone is trying to do his work as effectively as possible, and when he makes every effort to be on good terms with everyone, does he not come as close to God as if he were sitting there like a blockhead squinting at his watch?

On the last day, we spent three hours in mental prayer. All at one stretch! The time passed more quickly than the 30 minutes of the first day. Was it a matter of training and practice? No, six days cannot transform a person so completely on the strictly physiological-psychological level. I am inclined to believe that what happened to me was this: I had regained a hunger for God that impels to mental prayer.

Finding a place for this "thing" in my day

It was at that "House of Prayer" that I discovered the reason why I gave up meditation. Mental prayer had become for me a kind of "thing" that I had somehow to fit into my daily schedule at all costs. The schedule came first. My life governed my prayer.

Suddenly the perspective was reversed. I saw that it was hunger for God that constituted me as a man. I realized that this hunger (and hence mental prayer) must govern my life. There are certain Psalms that say a great deal more to me now than when I read them at an earlier time:

"My soul thirsts for God, the God of life" (Ps 42:2).

"God, you are my God, I am seeking you,

my soul is thirsting for you, my flesh is longing for you" (Ps 63:1).

"My heart and my flesh sing for joy

to the living God" (Ps 84:2).

Obviously, these faith-filled insights and this lyricism do not fit in very well with what we call "real" life. I became aware of that as soon as I got home from the "House of Prayer!" In any event, ever since that time I have always been able to find 30 minutes every day for mental prayer.

I must admit I also came to understand there is more than one kind of meditation! That is why it is probably better to speak of "mental prayer" (although I notice that zen is bringing the word "meditation" back into favor). This word indicates something that is broader in scope, more flexible, and definitely more appealing than traditional meditation.

Yet even if I succeed in restoring daily meditation to a place of honor in your eyes by making it tend toward mental prayer, I know the great mass of arguments that can be marshaled against it.

It is Copernican

In any case, this is the way I see it. Unless we *first* adopt the frame of mind of the Copernican revolution, any discussion of the "pro's and con's of daily meditation" is futile. We would be missing the point of the true problem. It is not a matter of finding time for "something more" in my day or of being initiated into a "spiritual technique." It concerns the all-encompassing sense I want to give to my life.

Either hunger for God is the sun around which I organize everything in my life, or else God is just one object among others orbiting the very crowded firmament of my life. Wouldn't you say that's a Copernican approach?

Now, you may have been startled when I said that hunger for God is what constitutes us as human persons. And yet it is the oft-repeated *"Fecisti nos ad te*—You have made us for yourself." Basically, we are turned toward God. In its deepest wellsprings, our being, a continuous creation of God, is totally a "vocation," a reaching out toward the plenitude to which God calls it, the fullness that will be God.

I suppose everybody accepts this in theory, but without going so far as to accept a behavioral pattern that would really be quite simple to discern. We are too willing to allow the *ad Deum*—turning toward God, which should be the creative force of our life, to be trampled on, encumbered, camouflaged, by a daily routine organized around other imperatives. As a result, when we are faced with making a resolution to engage in prayer we automatically try to find a place for it in our life *as we are now living it,* when we should instead *begin* by examining the fundamental idea on which we are building our life.

"I and God? Oh! No!"

I was trying to present these ideas to a group of friends. Nicholas exploded: "If you go on, I'm going to start shouting: 'I have only my own soul to save!' You are sinking into individualistic bigotry. 'I and God?' And what about the others?"

After a whole era of "I and God," we have finally become completely involved with "the others." We have no trouble saying that what constitutes a human person is fraternal love. Jesus is seen as being essentially "the man for others." That is correct, but it could

9

tend to become a mutilation, a diminishment. The entire Gospel cries out that Jesus has truly been "the man for others," but it was always *in the love of the Father.* And so I said to Nicholas:

"It's ridiculous to set our hunger for God in opposition to our concern for others. If you want to be 'a man for others,' never tire of asking yourself what kind of a man you want to offer them. You can be sure they won't hate anyone who hungers for God! Were Francis of Assisi, Theresa of Avila, and so many others individualistic bigots? And what about Madeleine Delbrêl, the apostle to the Marxist city? Do you know what she said? 'My Beloved, you will always be measured against this fascination, this consuming obsession with our trifles.' That is the choice we are making. It is not a choice between God and our brothers and sisters, but between God and our obsessions with trifles. And these obsessions do not always lead us toward our brothers and sisters!"

When mental prayer is seen to be in opposition to the apostolic life (and this is happening more and more!), I can readily see why prayer is conceived as time stolen from generous action on the human plane. But mental prayer is not just "a fleeting moment." It colors the whole life of those who hunger for God. And these lives always bear the hallmark of a hunger to serve others. Besides, the converse is true. The will to serve others better has led many to mental prayer.

But we need this "fleeting moment"

In order to "soar toward God" with our whole being, in order to enter into the spirit of mental prayer and dwell in it, we must have a very special daily encounter with God. Everyone who has had experience in this area agrees. But I don't think the point is adequately made that the time of mental prayer and the daily routine of our life must be "of a piece," homogenous. This is indispensable. I insist on this because it bears on what caused me to give up meditation.

The reason was this: my mental prayer had become too heterogeneous from a daily life organized *in a different spirit.*

Genuine (and persisting!) mental prayer can be nothing else than the most intense moment of a continual hunger for God. There is interaction between the two: hunger for God impels to mental prayer, and mental prayer intensifies our hunger for God which, in turn, leads us to rewarding and deepening periods of mental prayer.

Saint Augustine used to say something like this: "You seek in order to find; what you find impels you to seek." That is mental prayer when it is time spent by someone who, both before and afterwards, is in his or her very being "a soaring toward God." It cannot be anything else. Otherwise, mental prayer would consist in letting go of "real" life for 30 minutes of unreality, and then returning to what is believed to be "real" life.

Before determining to resume mental prayer, the big step to take is to accept *"You have made me for yourself"* as a *genuine reality,* as the central truth, the sun of your life. It will not be easy to live out. Concretely, it signifies that I want all of my life of prayer (whether private or liturgical) to be a reunion with God. It means that I want to go about every task without letting go of God, and to give myself to my brothers and sisters with God's own love. These desires can truly be called the *state of mental prayer,* the climate of mental prayer. And in this climate, as you can discover through experience, it is quite easy to find 30 minutes a day for mental prayer.

Far from being an immersion in unreality, our times of mental prayer can then be seen as the *most real moments of our life.*

This is the surest point of departure for daily mental prayer. I speak from experience. It was the day I understood the extreme realism of the moments devoted to mental prayer that I was eager to resume it. And now I wonder if anything could ever wrest me away from it. The rare occasions when I was filled once again with the itch to do ten other *very urgent* things rather than *waste* these 30 minutes, the whole day was spent in confusion and unreality. That "fleeting moment" makes normal men and women of us again. Normal according to faith, of course. But what other normalcy would we want to pursue?

Let us give him this gift

We shall talk at length about how we are to spend those 30 minutes. But first of all we want to see clearly why we give this moment of prayer to God. Here's the answer: so that he can keep us, day after day, turned toward him, filled with a great hunger for him. We have said almost everything about mental prayer when we define it as the most intense expectation of a contact with God, so as not to lose too much of this contact during the rest of the day.

I have used the word "expectation." I can't refrain from putting you on your guard against a false and very harmful idea. That is to imagine we go to mental prayer with the intention of racking our brains and simply in order to reach out and take hold of God, of the mysteries and energies of God. We go to mental prayer in order to let God work on us. There is no one so poor as the person who knows why he or she is going to mental prayer.

Our only riches consist of this fleeting moment, these 30 minutes we are about to give to God. Even so, there is something about this to make us dream. We have been so eager to give something to God. And there is indeed something we can give him. We can come before him every single day with this gift of 30 minutes. Come now, how many imperious reasons do we have for playing the miser with God?

OF WHAT USE IS PRAYER, ANYWAY?

If anyone asked me: "Of what use is prayer, anyway?" would I have a convincing answer to give? Some new ideas are going around these days about prayer. How have they affected me?

Sister Michèle, in her thirties, tells me she can't stand the tiresome repetition of: "We've *got* to pray! Do you pray well? What is your prayer life like? Are you faithful to your devotional exercises?" She says: "I have been given too many nudges to pray. I've come to link prayer with duty, with boredom. I have to get out of that rut. I'm hungry for a life with God."

We mustn't ask for anything any more?

J.J. (John Jerome), a young assistant pastor, confessed that the idea of taking a moment out of the day to pray frightens him.

— I'm afraid of this lull, this void that, I can't help feeling, is a waste of time. It's so artificial. I say what to whom? Must I really invent a presence of God for myself? A conversation with him? I prefer to let him see me act, reach out to others, solve problems. If you're united to God, if you give yourself generously to everyone, then your whole life is a prayer, isn't it?

— You're united to God? You give yourself to everyone?

— No, I was just bluffing. I don't know what to think any more. I would like to live closer to God, live in a state of prayer, but without praying. I can't get myself to recite Psalms that do not gibe with my feelings at that particular moment. When, during the celebration of the Eucharist, I say: "Let us pray," I have the sensation I am lying. I would need to stop for a long time, long enough to recapture a presence, a presence to myself, a presence to God. I would need to sense, together with the people who are there, that we are really going to say something to the Lord. God allows us to speak to him; he's willing to listen! That's extraordinary. But how can we help making it commonplace? As for meditation. . . . All the spiritual books bore me, even the Gospel. I've gone over them so many times.

— We can remain there, just to be imbued with God, just to adore. That's the way the young people are praying now, at Taizé and elswhere.

— Yes, the prayer of adoration is the only one that seems immune to debate. But you know me. I begin to think of everything I have to do. I ask God all sorts of things. And then I say to myself: "And why don't you get to work yourself?" Can we be sure that God wants us to come to him as beggars?

After J.J. had gone, I read for a little while, then I picked up my breviary. It opened at Psalm 123:

"I lift my eyes to you,

. . .

eyes like the eyes of slaves
fixed on their master's hand.

. . .

so our eyes are fixed on Yahweh our God,
for him to have pity on us. . . ."

It's the prayer of a beggar. And what of it? What has gotten into us to make us afraid of being beggars before God? It's true that we seem to be better able all the time to make a go of it by ourselves. But in what? Surely we are not making a success of living to the full, living by love, living (am I afraid to say it?) in holiness. It's not the prayer of petition that we must call into question, but what

14

we are asking for. What are the things we shall *always* have to pray for?

As if we were seeing the invisible

Chantal, 18 years old, from rural France, active in the French Catholic youth movement.

— Now that the chaplains dress like the other guys, it's easy to see which priests are men of God and which ones are just "pals." But, I've got plenty of pals. What I'm looking for in a priest is a way of reacting that forces me to think that there's something else besides our daily routine of life.

We priests are expected to be witnesses to the invisible. Obviously, our expertise on this point has been exaggerated. Every baptized person belongs to two worlds. Better still, every baptized person must look at the things of life with such faith-filled eyes that he can decipher another reality present and already a beginning of eternity. But isn't it quite normal to expect every priest to have this penetrating vision?

We should surprise others by our manner of sometimes being elsewhere, "enraptured," or strangely firm of purpose, as Moses is described in the Epistle to the Hebrews: "he held to his purpose like a man who could see the Invisible" (Hb ll:27). You must have noticed that people demand of us things that are apparently contradictory: they want us to be like everybody else, but not like everybody else. Not unreal, but not insipid.

A young activist in the French Catholic worker movement was telling me that she had gone to visit an elderly invalid woman, and they had prayed together. The old lady said to her: "When the pastor comes to see me, he talks to me just like anybody else. I'm expecting something more. It must embarrass him to talk about God."

I tried to explain to this young girl that a priest has a certain reserve, a certain discretion that prevents him from imposing on others a

15

conversation about God or a prayer. He's trying to share the human aspect of the other person's life rather than ramming religion down his or her throat.

The girl responded:

— A priest does not ram artificial platitudes down people's throats when he has a good relationship with God.

And that, I think, pinpoints the problem of prayer. Why should we pray? To continually strengthen our relationship with the *invisible* God. It is our fight to keep company with God *whom we do not see.*

Prayer is always ambiguous

I know, prayer is not our only relationship with God. Read Chapter 25 of Matthew: "You were keeping me company when you did this or that for a brother in misfortune." We keep company with God in our brothers, we keep company with him when we study theology and spirituality. But why should we refuse to keep him company through prayer? Fear of the unreal? Allow myself encounters only with myself or with a god of my own invention? That's surely something to check into. The "doubts" that have been hovering over prayer for some time now make us more demanding with respect to two fundamental points: *I am making contact with whom?* and *What am I asking?*

We can no longer refuse to see that prayer is always ambiguous. Is it an act of courage or cowardice? Is it narcissism or the will to give oneself more completely? The label "spiritual exercise" sometimes tends merely to cloak our fears of life and a way of sitting on the sidelines. "I'll pray for you!" has too often come to sound like: "I'll do nothing at all for you."

Yet at the bottom of the most depressing list of the wrong ways to pray, there will always be this certitude: *In order to go forward in life "as if we saw the invisible," we have to pray.* It is easy for us to cling to the visible world. That is what our senses are for. They are avid and busy. Zest for life constantly tends to eliminate prayer.

Clinging to the invisible world is a battle we don't like to fight. We are too quick to say we are going to "see things in faith" and "act in faith." But who would dare claim that the crossing of this frontier is easy? Prayer is a means of forcing the passage. Prayer is faith in the act of fighting in order to cling to the invisible. To pray is always to proclaim there is *something else* besides the visible world around us.

Going to the root of prayer

When our conscience is bothering us with respect to "our life of prayer," we are tempted to reinflate fervors of long ago. We call to mind the epoch of obligatory meditation, the ubiquitous rosary, the unfailing breviary, and Mass "to be said with greater attention."

Perhaps we need to delve deeper, go beyond all forms of prayer in order to reach the very root of prayer: *I want to pray because I thirst for God.*

With this starting point, we more easily come back to the necessary forms of prayer. We come back to them in a spirit of freedom. W. ... will resume meditating. X. ... will strive toward mental prayer. Y. ... will discover prayer on the agenda. Z. ... will passionately seek the Lord in the Gospel lived day by day.

Roger, a priest for thirty years and a chaplain, says:

— As for me, I pray in the street. Morning and night I have a long way to walk. I come across a prostitute, a drunkard, a couple of lovers, a mother burdened with kids and errands, people who are cheerful and others who are worried, the elderly who are merely surviving. I say: "Lord, what are you doing in this world? And what am I doing? What is life for this man, for that woman?"

When we are obsessed by this twofold necessity: of not letting go of God and not losing our lucidity on life, questions about the forms of prayer are very secondary. We can become quietly traditional, or we can be creative. It will always be something that is alive, that is earnestly sought. We are no longer making believe we are praying, we are discussing with God the way Job did. We are walking with God on our right hand, the way the Psalms dare to say it:

"I keep Yahweh before me always,
for with him at my right hand
nothing can shake me." (Ps 16:8)

To know you even in the darkness of night

All this commotion about "the death of God" must at least have shattered our way of imagining God and likewise our assurance when we spoke about him, about who he is, and what he wants.

If God is God, then we can know of him only what he has been able to reveal to us in human words and in the histories of men and women. Now, our prayers simply seek to wrest from God a groping proximity to him in the night. These encounters are often the wrestling of a Jacob.

Jacob:—"I will not let you go unless you bless me!"

The Man: "Your name shall no longer be Jacob
                    but Israel, because you have fought
                    with God as one fights with men."

Jacob:—"I beg you, tell me your name."

The Man: "Why do you ask my name?"

(cf. Gn 32:25-30)

Why? Because I want to know you as much as any man can know God here on earth, to know you in faith, in the darkness of the night. You have willed that we should live for a few years this mystery of your presence-absence that makes us groan: *You are so far, Lord!* You answer: *I am very close to you.* What else is prayer except my thirst and your coming?

18

A BOUNDLESS TRUST IN GOD

We are going to live together

Prayer is a kind of gamble on the way we are going to live our life. It is a choice to live every part of our life with God. Thanks, of course, to what we are continually wresting from him.

The moment we try this living-together, the gamble is won! Once we have begun to live each day in a continuous and loving discussion with the Lord, with a boundless trust in him, I doubt we can ever again let go of this way of living. And as a result prayer no longer presents a real problem. There are merely questions of how well we are progressing as listeners, how faithfully we keep our eyes fixed on God, and above all whether ours is an ever more fantastic trust in what God can do with our personality and our life.

I did not use the words *boundless trust* and *fantastic trust* simply to be lyrical. I say it because when we speak of prayer that really tells the whole story.

A boundless trust in God

The importance (and the difficulty!) of *really* trusting when we pray is something I discovered when studying the spiritual doctrine of Saint Thérèse of Lisieux. She built up her holiness on this foundation: *trusting God boundlessly.* And then going on to prove it!

After all, it's not very hard to think and to say we place our trust in God. But when our backs are to the wall, we give up.

Whenever someone has told me: "I'm not doing so well with prayer any more," whenever I have gone through prayer-crises myself, I have always come to the same conclusion. The root of the matter is that *we don't believe that prayer can really change our life.* We have not plunged fully into prayer because we didn't dare jump headlong into a mad trust in God.

As long as we hesitate, as long as we merely *add* a little more prayer to our life just to play it safe, but with a trust made of tinplate, we cannot truly experience prayer. We remain among those who get bored with prayer before even trying it, who meander among theories, who are forever searching for methods and for gurus.

No, there's no getting around it. Our current forms of prayer are not sick. It's our underlying trust that is sick. We keep asking: *What difference will my prayer make anyway?*

Granted, I'll never be able to see the difference. But I shall be given the strength to accept, to overcome. My personality, my prayer, and the power of God—these three weave the fabric of my life, even if I cannot easily discern the various patterns in it. I shall be able to pray well only when, without seeing, I believe that when I pray I am doing something that is mysteriously decisive.

Do I believe in prayer when I pray?

A diagnosis of my prayer must consist in observing the power of my faith when I engage in this action which unfortunately is so easily noncommittal.

It is the power with which I show God that I really expect something from *this* prayer that links my life to his power. But there is another reason that explains why prayer is sometimes given up. If my trust is weak, I have not really bound myself, opened myself, to the power of God. I remain limited to my own petty means, and this soon becomes apparent in my behavior. Vexed, I think: what difference does prayer make? But I am judging only an appearance of prayer. I am judging *a prayer that does not believe.*

Look at the problem as we may from every angle, the answer always emerges. There is a power that God is ready to put into action the instant a person prays, *but in the very measure that this person believes in it and puts his heart into it.* It may be surprising but it is true: before God acts, he awaits the assaults of our trust. Jesus never tired of teaching this lesson to us by describing some very boring people. We have to bore God, we have to pester him (cf. Lk 18:5).

But we are far from such stubborn, demanding prayer. I have often thought about that when meditating on the persistent widow and the troublesome friend.

Jesus told this parable: "Suppose one of you has a friend and goes to him in the middle of the night to say, 'My friend, lend me three loaves, because a friend of mine on his travels has just arrived at my house and I have nothing to offer him'; and the man answers from inside the house, 'Do not bother me. The door is bolted now, and my children and I are in bed; I cannot get up to give it to you'. I tell you, if the man does not get up and give it to him for friendship's sake, persistence will be enough to make him get up and give his friend all he wants" (Lk 11:5-8).

"Then he told them a parable about the need to pray continually and never lose heart. 'There was a judge in a certain town who had neither fear of God nor respect for man. In the same town there was a widow who kept on coming to him and saying, "I want justice from you against my enemy!" For a long time he refused, but at last he said to himself: "Maybe I have neither fear of God nor respect for man, but since she keeps pestering me I must give this widow her rights, or she will persist in coming and worry me to death."

"And the Lord said: 'You notice what the unjust judge has to say? Now will not God see justice done to his chosen who cry to him day and night even when he delays to help them?' " (Lk 18:1-7).

This prayer-relationship between God and us is disconcerting. Why do we have to keep insisting so much? And what tangible results do we obtain? All this remains a very mysterious domain. We are no longer dealing man-to-man. There is no way to compare this with our other relationships. And finally, I have a hard time understanding what God can do when I pray.

Help me to believe that much!

Jesus expressed surprise at this sort of hesitancy. Read, for example, the account of the healing of the epileptic child (Mk 9:14-29). The wretched father's request triggered a reaction of impatience in Jesus that is almost strange. "You faithless generation. How much longer must I be with you? How much longer must I put up with you?" (Mk 9:19). Then the frightened father explained to him: "Your disciples didn't have the power to cure my child. But you, if you can do anything. . . ."

Again Jesus expressed displeasure:

— "If you *can?* Everything is possible for anyone who has faith." (Mk 18:23).

Prayer and the impossible. That's it! A dive into *inordinate* trust, trust beyond any human measure. The father sees it clearly. He stammers something sublime that we shall continue to cry out as long as there are men and women facing the power of God.

— "I do have faith. Help the little faith I have!" (Mk 8:24)

I remember at a Bible-sharing on this Gospel, a young woman said something that set us all to thinking.

This is what she said:

— What a vast difference there is between this intense prayer which does violence to our own hesitation to believe what God can do, and our "Let us pray" 's! Our prayers almost inevitably become a kind of routine droning, without any real determination to wrest something from God. This gets us into the habit of praying weakly. And that is how we end up not praying at all.

There is no doubt that the great majority of weak prayers gradually undermine the heartfelt intensity with which we should approach God. Of all the difficulties I have had in prayer, this seems to me the most formidable. We maim our sense of prayer in pseudo-prayers. "In your prayers do not babble as the pagans do, for they think that by using many words they will make themselves heard" (Mt 6:7).

The insistent prayer that makes God listen is not lengthy prayer but prayer "that believes in him." We pray seriously only when we have a very lofty idea of what prayer is.

As I have already mentioned, this idea, this conviction tends to wear thin in everyone, and in me first of all. Periodically I have to reactivate my reasons for praying. To this end, I use a very simple means.

It's God who tells me to pray

I try to relive the shock I felt when I "listened," as I had never listened before, to the words, "pray continually."

And so I come back to Luke: "Then Jesus told them a parable about the need to pray continually and never lose heart" (Lk 18:1). "Stay awake, praying at all times" (Lk 21-36). Or to Paul: "pray constantly" (1 Th 5:17), etc. And I pause to reflect on what will always be the strongest, the most unshakable reason for praying: *prayer, constant prayer, is something that God asks of us.*

I can quibble over the advice of my fellow men. But who is talking to me here? Who is commanding me? Someone who wants the very best for me as no one else can. God himself in his wisdom and his love. I weigh the evidence: God knows himself, God knows me. He knows what he can and wants to do with me. And he needs this relationship of prayer between us. He tells me: Pray!

23

God obviously has his own reasons for wanting to work with me *in this way,* for joining his power to my shortcomings *in this way.* It is not useless to delve into these reasons and to discover the necessity for prayer *from my own human point of view.*

But at the wellspring of the rivers of ideas and words on prayer, I'll never find anything more reliable and more convincing than what God our Father himself says: *Believe me, son, Pray!*

God speaks to me through Jesus, *who came to reveal to us what is important if we want to live.* But we find this command in the Bible from beginning to end. To live close to the Bible is to live close to prayer. It means being close to men of prayer, to examples of prayer.

In the Book of Psalms there is even a history of the prayer-relationship between God and ourselves, a vast rainbow of cries, laments, explanations, thank-you's, that God himself has given me so that I may know what pleases him in the prayer of a man or woman.

Once I have been imbued with Biblical prayer, it's up to me to invent my own prayer-relationship. But in all of this, I must never forget that I pray *first of all* because God tells me to pray.

"MAKE ME WANT TO PRAY"

I was talking about prayer with Jim. This is what he had to say:
— Every time I began to pray again, it never lasted. Life always got the upper hand. I can see why: I was never completely convinced. That's my problem. If you want to help me, make me want to pray, convince me.

I could understand what he was saying. I went through the same difficulties in prayer. I still have them when I begin to stray again toward prayer *in the abstract,* prayer *in general,* toward the theoretical reasons why it is necessary to pray.

I discovered that this is a common mistake. We discuss *"prayer in general,"* as if we Christians were talking about any kind of prayer.

The fact is that it is not a matter of "praying," of "praying better," the way it seems to be, because "it is necessary to pray" or, for example, because we are slipping into activism.

It's a matter of being Christian. To live a Christian life means to keep looking at Christ and trying to live like him. Is that naive? Maybe, but let's follow this logic to the end. Why are we always making (more or less conscious) choices as to what we want to imitate in Christ? We watch him *love.* Why don't we watch him *pray?*

Jesus experienced *the need* to pray. And I don't need to pray? But what exactly do I want? *To be me* or to follow Christ? On what grounds can I decide I'm going to follow him *on this matter* but not *on some other matter.* I'll follow him when it comes to brotherly love, but not when it comes to prayer.

I used to be like Jim. I wasn't the sort of person drawn to prayer. Nonetheless I sensed there was a major choice involved here. That's why I used to beg: *"Make me want to pray."* One day, someone said to me:

— Why don't you look at Jesus? He experienced the need to pray. Believe me, that's the most powerful incentive to make anybody want to pray.

Jesus needed a special time devoted to solitary prayer

In the tumultuous eighth chapter of Saint John, in the midst of very bitter scrimmages with some Jews, a patch of blue suddenly pierced through the stormy skies. Jesus allowed himself to make a poignant admission:

"I do nothing of myself. What the Father has taught me is what I preach. ... He who sent me is with me. He has not left me to myself. For I always do what pleases him" (Jn 8:28-29).

A short while before, the Jews—aggressive but visibly troubled—had asked: "Where is your Father?" Jesus had answered: "If you did know me, you would know my Father as well" (Jn 8:19).

It is clear that a man has walked our earth who lived an extraordinary union with God. A constant, perfect union (seeking *always* to please the Father). And this union is so close that to look at this man is to see God himself (but what a penetrating gaze this requires!).

Well now, keeping before you this picture of the Son so intimately united to his Father, try to read Saint Luke. You will discover statements like these:

"Now it was about this time that he went out into the hills to pray; and he spent the whole night in prayer to God" (Lk 6:12).

"Large crowds would gather to hear him . . . , but he would always go off to some place where he could be alone and pray" (Lk 5:15-16).

Since I was told: *"Take a good look at Jesus praying,"* I always see two things: Jesus lived constantly united to his Father, and nevertheless he had to pull himself away from the work of proclaiming the Kingdom and go off by himself to pray.

We look silly, don't we, the way we get bored with prayer and raise objections to prayer: "There's no need for a special time of solitary prayer. It is enough to live united to God and to do what we have to do. Besides, praying in seclusion is to run away. It's better to serve."

Instead of arguing, let's look at Jesus again. Saint Luke is very exact: Jesus does not turn away from the crowd or from his Apostles in order to forget them in his search for intimacy with his Father. He leaves them only in order to serve them better.

After his baptism that initiated his mission, Jesus prayed (cf. Lk 3:21). Before the most crucial choice of The Twelve, "he went out into the hills to pray" (Lk 6:12). It was after he had been praying alone that he asked the famous question: "Who do you say I am?" (Lk 9:18-20).

There is no question here of a prayer of escapism, but on the contrary we find a continual concern with his mission. Later he would say to Peter: *"I have prayed for you, Simon, that your faith may not fail"* (Lk 22:32). And when we think of his forty days in the desert before he went into action, we can easily see that his prayer in seclusion was also a prayer of combat (cf. Mt 4:2 ff.).

Entering into Jesus' prayer

When we are looking for strong reasons why we should pray, why not take this shortcut? *Jesus needed to pray.*

Unless we start out by meditating on Jesus' own prayer we always run the risk of building some sort of prayer life that is not "Christian" at all. I mean on something other than the reasons Christ himself had for praying.

Then our prayer inevitably becomes the prayer of our own little personal histories, of our unending examens, of our narrow petitions, which (we must admit) are never answered. It's so easy to destroy our desire to pray in that climate of prayer!

But the instant I look at Jesus, the horizon changes. One might even say there is a quasi-total upheaval in our outlook. Jesus says: *"When you want to pray, ask: Father, your kingdom come!"* (cf. Mt 6:10, Lk 11:2).

On the spot, I then enter into Jesus' own prayer. He lived what he taught. I am no longer in the realm of theory ("Prayer is necessary"), but I have embarked upon the very concrete adventure of living like Jesus.

Jesus joined his love for the Father and his love for his brothers and sisters into a perfect unity. Not as though they were two separate realities, but as two loves that nurture one another. When he went alone to the Father it was *in order to think about his mission.* But when his brothers experienced success, he turned at once to the Father: *"I bless you, Father, Lord of heaven and earth, for hiding these things from the learned and the clever and revealing them to mere children"* (Lk 10:21).

Prayer manifestly played a very important role in the success of a life as totally unified as that of Jesus. And I am called to enter into this efficacious, powerful prayer. Not the prayer of theories and psychologies. It must be "Christian" prayer, the prayer of Jesus. I know that I must announce, continue, and manifest the love of Jesus through my own life. I must arrive at another conviction. I must also announce, continue, and manifest his prayer by my own prayer.

The most powerful model of prayer

Jesus' prayer is simple, extremely concrete. It is always an effort to discover the Father's will and to be immersed in it. In the face of a difficult demand which filled him with fear, he prayed. He who had dared to affirm: "I always do what pleases him" almost gave up. It's in a moment like that that we must watch him pray if we want to see what a genuine Christian confrontation of prayer really means—what prayer can wrest from God.

"Abba (Father)! Everything is possible for you. Take this cup away from me. But let it be as you, not I, would have it" (Mk 14:36).

This is the most powerful model of prayer. I shall have entered into Jesus' prayer when my own prayers have this accent. Everything is here.

And first of all, we see that we are not expected to cringe before a potentate. We are always allowed to begin with "Father"! Christian prayer exists only in a climate of love. I begin by reaffirming, as Jesus shows me, that I am loved: *"Abba (beloved Father)!"* It will sometimes be very hard to do. But if we do not begin by placing ourselves once again in a climate of love, then our prayer is not *like Christ's.*

I reaffirm my trust: *"Everything is possible for you!"* Jesus has told us often enough that without this trust there's little use coming before God.

Not that! I can't do it!

And *like Jesus,* I dare to express my gropings, my fears: If I don't reach down to the roots of my fears, what do I think I am doing when I say I am praying? And what power can my cry have?

But I need so desperately to look at Jesus! To know that there was a moment when even he, so intimately united to his Father, made a distinction between what he wanted and what his Father wanted. It was in prayer that he confronted this crisis, it was through prayer that he struggled to make their two wills coincide. What an example! Jesus was never closer to us. He went so far as to assume the fear of what God can demand of a man. But as for us, this fear drives us away from prayer. Jesus, for his part, takes his fear into his prayer, he does not let go of his Father. In the presence of this deeply troubled

Jesus, I can understand that prayer is sometimes an intense moment, a decisive moment in the life of a man or a woman.

It is at such a moment that Jesus said what was hardest for him: *"Let it be as you, not I, would have it!"* The Gospel text is quickly read. But what terrible minutes must have passed between *"Take this cup away from me!"* and *"Let it be as you would have it!"* Where could we learn better that praying is not playacting but wresting from God what we need in order to do what he expects of us.

THE SPIRIT IS ALWAYS GIVEN TO THOSE WHO PRAY

Excerpt from a letter from Jack, a student:

— I've always found it hard to pray, but right now my will to pray is about to collapse in the face of arguments against it. For example, I hear things like this: "The Gospel affirms our prayers are answered. It's easy to see that's not true!" It is also said (and I have been saying so for a long time): "What possible use can prayer have? God knows everything. And in any event, he's not going to change his mind because of me." And to top it all, even "spiritual" people think it's shameful always to be asking. When we pray we are to adore, give thanks. So much for poor old prayer of petition!

"Poor old prayer of petition?" What I say is: "Great prayer of petition!" I have often been stymied by the unbelievable words of Mark 11:24, but now I realize it is one of the most powerful and vital passages of the Gospel.

"I tell you therefore: everything you ask and pray for, believe that you have it already, and it will be yours!"

Obviously, we think of the tons of prayers that have been hurled at God and not been answered. We don't dare say Jesus is speaking here like a candidate for public office. But there's no denying that life cruelly contradicts its promises. We are tempted to give up. It's too good to be true.

Not at all! Let us believe these words of the Gospel. And put up a valiant fight to discover what lies behind such a disconcerting affirmation.

First of all, let us reflect on the vast and impressive array of Gospel sayings on the efficacy of prayer. The simplest approach is by way of Luke, Chapter 11.

The disciples watch Jesus praying and they say to him: "Teach us to pray." Jesus' answer is *the Lord's Prayer.* Here we have a whole collection of "give me's"! It seems reasonable that if Jesus, as the teacher of prayer, commands us to ask, the prayer of petition can't be so inferior.

And now Jesus is going to show what this prayer obtains. Providing it is persistent (cf. Lk 11:5-9):
"So I say to you: Ask, and it will be given to you. . . .
For the one who asks always receives. . . .
What father among you would hand his son a stone
when he asked for bread? . . . .
how much more will the heavenly Father give. . . ."(Lk 11:9-13)

Give what? In the parallel passage (Mt 7:11), Matthew says that our Father will give *good things* to those who pray. Luke says: "The heavenly Father will give *the Holy Spirit* to those who ask him!" (Lk 11:13).

It took me a long time to discover this is one of the great secrets of the prayer of petition. And that is precisely why petition is such a lofty prayer.

If I pray well, that is to say, persistently and with *filial* trust, I will receive the Spirit. (Obviously my prayer must not be an attempt to make use of the great Magician, or to beg mercy of the great Tyrant, for I am before my loving Father.)

But I was asking for a sunny day for the parish bazaar, I was not asking for the Holy Spirit!

The Spirit attunes us to God

I think we are reminded of another saying about the link between the prayer of petition and the Spirit:

"The Spirit too comes to help us in our weakness. For when we cannot choose words in order to pray properly, the Spirit himself expresses our plea in a way that could never be put into words, and God who knows everything in our hearts knows perfectly well what he means, and that the pleas of the saints expressed by the Spirit are according to the mind of God" (Rm 8:26-27).

To pray according to the mind of God! That is a strong beam of light on the prayer of petition. God has great plans for his Creation, his Kingdom, his People, for each of us. *He has great plans for me.*

I come toward God with my piddling five-and-dime petitions. For example, I ask him to relieve my headache so I can write this page lucidly. The important thing about my petition is that it reorients me in the direction of God. I am usually very distracted from God. *I live my life alone,* and hence within narrow limits and in humiliating weakness. Even my smallest petition, if I make it correctly, brings me back to God *in very truth.* For I am what he expects of me: a trusting son or daughter who is asking something from his/her loving Father.

A petition that brings us back to God is truly worthwhile! I realize that my words are useless to God, for he knows everything: "Your Father knows what you need before you ask him" (Mt 6:8). But my words are not useless for me. My prayers of petition can be the great school of my desires.

I start out with: "Give us a sunny day tomorrow, make John Mark pass his entrance exam into junior high, help my father to endure his cancer, make Ginny successful in her efforts to start a youth group in her parish, give Bangladesh a chance to become a viable nation. . . ." God sees that I am someone who is asking, and asking with *filial* trust. So he can give the Spirit to me.

33

Then comes the great upheaval: the Spirit, who is God's Breath, *God's "Aspiration,"* breathes into me aspirations that are ever more closely in tune with God's plans.

When I ask, the Spirit can transform me

This won't come about automatically. But I shall come closer to one of Jesus' great demands which governs every prayer of petition: "Seek first the kingdom of God and his justice" (cf. Mt 6:33). And I shall find a new delight in two petitions which are so often uttered carelessly: "Your kingdom come, your will be done" (Mt 6:10; Lk 11:2).

Let us review these words: "I tell you therefore: everything you ask and pray for, believe that you have it already, and it will be yours" (Mk 11:24). Seen in isolation, this passage is unusable. It must be placed within the context of Jesus' whole way of thinking. He is totally filled with the Spirit, and his human petitions coincide with the Father's plans ("I always do what pleases him" Jn 8:29). At the very least, the petitions finally coincide with the plans ("Let your will be done, not mine" Lk 22:42). When Jesus says "everything you ask," the word "ask" necessarily has an accent of acceptance before the fact or of acceptance of God's plans for the future.

We can see the role of the prayer of petition in the life of a Christian. Not only does it constantly bring us back to God in a filial spirit; but under the action of the Spirit, *who is always given to the person who prays,* it shapes us in accordance with God's tastes and broadens us to the scope of his horizons. Without petitions, I remain a man *alone.* With my petitions, I am a man whom the Spirit can transform.

The irreducible mystery of the prayer of petition: our encounter with God

But a malaise, a doubt slips into my mind. So my prayer is simply my own effort focussed on myself? So God does not move, does not change anything? If I am suffering from cancer, it is because it was in God's great Plan? Amen! Then Mark 11:24 would mean: "Ask what God has decided from all eternity, and your prayer will be answered!"

Certain philosophers of prayer initiate us into the complicated and icy mechanism of a Plan that God completely integrated in advance, including my own prayers. I am only a robot who carries out the program of the super-powerful computer with which God decided everything once and for all.

At the other extreme is the belief that God can turn the order of the universe and the interplay of secondary causes topsy-turvy whenever he pleases in answer to prayer. "Grant that I may not have an automobile accident today."

These debates are rather boring, but we must not give up. We are facing the very mystery of our human condition: *our contact with God*.

The prayer of petition essentially brings this contact into question. Either our prayers are really efficacious or the Gospel is making fools of us. But they bring into play such a mysterious cooperation between God and ourselves that all we can say about it is this: God's eternal world comes into contact with the human world existing in time; and this contact occurs at the very place and moment when a man or woman turns to God and entreats him as a son or daughter.

The difficulty lies in imagining this joining of eternity and time. Here I far prefer the warmth of Mark 11:24 to the philosophers' analyses. The Gospel does not reveal a Computer-God to me, rather it reveals a living Creation in which everything is not already predetermined, in which sons and daughters can at this very moment make efficacious requests of their Father. It's up to him, the Eternal One, to see how our petitions made in time penetrate his eternity and act within it and upon it. There is an irreducible mystery in the prayer of petition, just as there is each time God works with us.

Does God answer our prayers?

We have to admit that these two flights of thought, one directed toward the gift of the Spirit and the other toward philosophers, has brought us a long way from modest requests for a sunny day for the parish bazaar. This was necessary. We had to clear away a few troublesome ideas relating to Mark 11:24. Now we are ready to confront the real question: Does God answer our petitions? Yes, but on two conditions. We have just seen the first of these conditions: we must allow ourselves to be moved by the Holy Spirit in order to achieve a mysterious joining of our life and God's will. And now we shall meditate on the second condition: We must pray with courage.

OUR DAILY LIFE IS THE MOST SACRED OF ALL

Life means waking up in the morning, going through the whole day until evening, and then beginning over again the next day. Everything we can imagine in the way of desires, thoughts, spirituality, and action comes down to what we do day after day, hour after hour. Our daily life is the most sacred human reality because that is where a man or woman comes to maturity. That is where saints are born.

I seem to be proclaiming platitudes with a pompous air. But I tend more and more to distrust the shocking lack of realism among Christians whenever someone speaks to them about prayer and the spiritual life. I had preached a retreat to a group of fifteen- and sixteen-year-old girls. Afterwards Catherine came up to thank me, beaming: *"Now I'm really going to live!"* A week later I happened to see her and inquired how the retreat was affecting her life. She gave me a puzzled look: *"What retreat?"* Then she caught herself: *"Oh! Of course, yes. It was so long ago!"* Nothing had changed in her daily life which had resumed its ordinary course.

Never link prayer to an easier life

Many prayers sound like something out of a fairy tale: "Lord, turn this pumpkin into a stagecoach!" When prayer drives me far from my real life, I allow myself to be consumed by reveries: "If only I didn't have these headaches! If only we had another pastor! If only our son had wanted to go into business!"

The grass is always greener next door. When I daydream like that, it always seems to me that if I had been situated in a different kind of life I could have been a terrific guy. My prayer suffers from these mirages. In one way or another, I am asking God to change my life through some kind of *magic*.

Nowadays almost everyone around me tends to pray and to have others pray that things may change at the least cost. After a year of outrageous loafing, a young man quietly asked me: "Please pray hard so that I'll pass my exams and graduate with my class."

This is obviously a caricature of prayer. At the other extreme, I found myself unable to say anything to a mother in deep misfortune. Her three-year-old child was dying. I thought of all this vanished happiness. I didn't dare speak of prayer. What could she ask for? She had told me her child was lost to her forever. I felt she was somehow expecting me to help her to live this reality. I didn't have any words because we are so accustomed to pray that certain things won't happen. We don't know how to pray for a way to live through the things that may indeed happen.

That's when I sensed suddenly and violently that we must destroy the mold that links prayer to a life preserved from misfortune, to the easier life.

A comparison comes to mind. People are constantly asking me for *easy* religious books. As I see it, this is a downturn from two points of view. First, as to the value of what one wants to read: easy religious books are often mediocre. And secondly, as to the reader's effort to nurture his or her faith. When I esteem and love someone, I recommend a difficult book. To love is not to make life easier, it is to help someone live more fully.

But after all, why would anyone ask God to let him or her live less fully? We are not asking this consciously. We are simply trying to ward off the obstacle, to exorcise fear through prayers which, if they were indeed answered, would lead us only to a life of ever greater capitulation. God will not listen to anyone who asks for a way of getting by without courage.

Pray for the grace to live out what seems to be stupid, revolting, complicated

When I find I am beginning to dream or to surrender, the breviary often awakens me with this cry: "The Lord is my strength!" I also make use of Theresa of Avila's saying: "God loves courageous people." He must not like those who escape from their difficult life in order to go and dream with him about *something else.* As my nephew expresses it, God cannot be my strength when I am walking not in my shoes but alongside them. My prayer as a *courageous* man must seek to draw God's strength into my real life. I shall ask only one thing: *"Lord, help me to live what I have to live through."*

Once again, under the triteness of formulas, I ask you to scrutinize the reversal of our perspectives: *we must expect everything from our daily life.*

I applied this idea to a visitor. Let's call her Sylvia. She was married, had two children, serious marital problems, and her menstrual periods were too irregular to allow her to use the temperature method of natural family planning. She lamented: "If only I didn't have this moral bugaboo!"

This is what I told Sylvia:

— It is precisely in this bugaboo that God is waiting for you to make you holy. Your hesitancy to use an artificial contraceptive, your disturbing search for what will be most conducive to fulfilling your fundamental obligation to love, that is already love of your husband and love of God. This bugaboo is actually the place of your battle and therefore of your prayer. Don't pray not to have any more bugaboos but pray to live the one you have as well as possible.

I realize such a frame of mind is hard to acquire because we are so terribly inclined to take refuge in all kinds of unreality. Here the lack of realism would consist in expecting this problem to disappear, a problem that Sylvia described as "repugnant." The very word betrays a lack of realism. We could take a minute here to examine our vocabulary: *"It's stupid! It's revolting. It's complicated. Why me?"* We must constantly counter these rejections with a realistic search: *"Amid all of this, how can I love?"*

Have I wandered too far from prayer? No, I think I am delimiting its real parameters, what I would readily call *spiritual realism:* wanting to live to the full, with the strength of God, what we are very concretely expected to live at this particular moment.

Daily life logjammed in the impossible

Obviously, we shall immediately run into *difficulties.* And yet we have still not entered the true terrain of prayer. When we have a toothache, we can go to the dentist. When we have to work with an irritating colleague, we can have recourse to patience and humor.

But take something like this. Last week a friend came to tell me that his wife, suddenly fascinated by an extremist religious sect, was dragging their three children along with her into her new religious belief. The man said: "I am living through a kind of nightmare. You knew what our home life was like. Can you imagine such a disaster?"

I am reminded also of a young husband who has just been informed that his wife has cancer. Sadly enough, all of us can add to the list of lives suddenly logjammed in the *impossible.*

There are other burdens that make us cry out: "Impossible!" Right now, I am hungry to live in God's presence, and I can't seem to do it. I say: "Lord, why is it so hard?" And what about the great dream we all have of becoming saints—why does it raise up such a mountain of impossibilities?

Now we are coming closer to true prayer! As long as we have not prayed for the strength to endure the impossible or to make the impossible succeed, we don't know what the Christian idea of prayer involves. *Prayer is working with God within the impossible.*

Then we call on God to come where he can and wants to come because someone is striving to live to the full what a human person must live. God did not create men and women to have them seek anything else than a human life. But that often means a heavily burdened life, and sometimes running into a stone wall.

To pray at such moments is to be exactly what we are meant to be: paupers and sons who want to go all the way, breaking the logjam by their prayers so they can release the flow of God's power they need so much.

"Though it seemed Abraham's hope could not be fulfilled, he hoped and he believed, and through doing so he did become *the father of many nations. . . .* Even the thought that his body was past fatherhood—he was about a hundred years old—and Sarah too old to become a mother, did not shake his belief. Since God had promised it, Abraham refused either to deny it or even to doubt it, but drew strength from faith and gave glory to God, convinced that God had power to do what he had promised" (Rm 4:18-21).

Faith filled Abraham with God's promise. This is not a matter of the Almighty's abstract power, but of the power God can exercise on our behalf when an impossibility arises in our life.

Mary is told she will have a child and she sees only that this is not possible. The angel says: Yes, *"for nothing is impossible to God"* (Lk 1:37). Jesus says: ". . .it will be hard for a rich man to enter the kingdom of heaven" (Mt 19:23). His hearers feel crushed under the burden of their lives: "Who can be saved, then?" Jesus answers with the opening words of our meditation: *"For men this is impossible; for God everything is possible"* (Mt 19:26). Let us add: Everything is possible to us with God, through prayer.

Our prayers of courage

It's up to us to keep trying. We asked ourselves a question: *How does God answer our petitions in our daily life?* Answer: By helping us to live in situations where we would normally give up praying, in situations where we would not normally take advantage of the opportunity to do something extraordinary. God answers our prayers of courage and he answers our prayers begging for courage! I won't have the courage to live through that, Lord, but with your help I want to live through it.

It would be useless to go any further into this, and it would even be a form of escapism. We simply have to turn our gaze back on our life, refuse to try to get out of whatever happens to be hard or even impossible, and keep telling ourselves that our chance of success lies right where we are and not elsewhere. Providing our prayer draws down the power of God upon us.

AM I MADLY IN LOVE WITH GOD?

Long ago I was taught to examine "my lives," the way a farmer divides his fields: my apostolate on one side, my spiritual life on the other. Nowadays we would add: "my human life."

Let's be farmers to the hilt and ask ourselves: what is my land worth? What is my value, my depth as a human person? And am I madly in love with God? Do I possess these two things? This requires a careful examination. For if I am indeed a person of deep human quality and if I love God madly, then *everything* in me will draw me to prayer, *everything* in me will impel me impatiently to apostolic action, *everything* in me will have human value.

We don't have three lives. That is a way of speaking that imprisons us in futile problems. How much time should I spend on the apostolate? How much time in prayer? How much time looking at TV?

Such an approach leads us to make of our spiritual life a specialized sector of our life as a whole, and the devaluation is disastrous. For then our spiritual life is reduced to a certain number of devotional exercises. And we emerge from them to go on to another kind of exercise called "the apostolate."

Peter who has been a priest 27 years responds:

— No, I don't go from my devotional exercises to apostolic work. *I have given up those spiritual exercises. It's a thing of the past. But can you offer me something better?*

To go after the fruits without worrying about the tree

Talking with this friend, I notice that he is still stymied by the old problem of the three lives. He speaks about his spiritual life that is increasingly "swallowed up" by apostolic action. He eagerly asks for advice on "how to pray better." He insists a great deal on his concern to "work out a balance between action, recreation, and prayer."

—But Peter, who is going to work out the balance? That's the real problem. What kind of a man are you *deep inside?* What do you really want? Where do you stand with God? You are not three men— an apostle, a man of prayer, and a man living an ordinary daily life. Wherever you are, whatever you are doing, you bring your whole self to it. Unless perhaps you are playing a role, creating a theatrical character when you pray, when you preach. But deep inside, you are just one very clear type of man who has a *very specific temperament and spirit.* That must be your first and foremost concern. Are you a man of character? Are you madly in love with God?

Now, such questions do not cover the whole problem. But everything depends on them. Hurray for apostolic action! But *who* is this apostle? Hurray for devotional exercises! But *who* is meditating? Hurray for efforts to be deeply involved in a human way! But *who* is this man eager to be involved? We tend to go after the fruits without worrying about the tree. Don't we do this to escape a much more terrible demand than the one to pray or to preside over a meeting? The leader of a youth group kept repeating at one of our meetings: "We've got to do this, and we've got to do that." I could hardly keep from asking: "But first of all, *who* are you? *Who* are we that we should do this and that?"

The need is not for a balance but for a change of heart

What is the terrible demand on us? It's not anything very unusual, but it frightens us so much that we prefer to keep examining how well we are balancing our activities rather than face the one action that would make us different beings, the action that would establish balance in our lives.

This is the first action Jesus called for in the Gospel of Mark: *"Repent, and believe the Good News"* (Mk 1:15). We are called to a change of heart, to a conversion of our whole being.

— We need to be converted? But we're being converted all the time!

— No.

We are constantly being invited to a change of heart. The occasion may be an encounter with a truly spiritual person, an illness, a book, a retreat. *In our thoughts* we outline the great conversion, but we turn back to our petty calculations: so much for God, so much for the apostolate, so much for me. We are not crazy. That is, we are not crazy about God.

Well then, what are we to do? Let us at least look at the stakes we are playing for. There is no part-time work for the Lord. Instead of calculating and working out a balance, it would be wiser to accept to be completely crazy. It would be better to flip and believe. To ask God (it's beyond our strength!) to take hold of us, turn us around, and finally make us men and women of faith. That's the only real prayer, or in any case it is the forerunner of all prayer that always bears within it every other kind of prayer: *Give me faith! Help me to believe!* If we can get over our fears and dare to shout this prayer with our whole being, God will take us at our word.

Let's not allow ourselves to be ensnared

It happened to John, to Mary Magdalene, to Paul, to Augustine, and to Francis. In one fell swoop. It will probably happen to us in

45

several stages. But we must think about it more than anything else. It is more important to cling desperately to this goal of fundamental conversion than to look around for various forms of prayer and for effective apostolic tactics. These things are important but only in the measure we are already turned around.

I realize I am writing my own condemnation. I have been stymied for so long before the terrible mystery of Christ's life. To see with blinding clarity that everything depends on an initial conversion, and not to *really* want to wrest this conversion from God. But I must go about my METIER D'ABOYEUR. What is required of us is not so many prayers, so many lectures, and so many sacraments. We are asked to change, to believe and to be madly in love with God. Then prayer is truly prayer and the fire in our hearts burns others.

Ephesians 4:17-24 is really meant for us

A change of heart means that we let go of a whole bundle of attitudes and take on new ones. There are no more powerful words on this subject than those in Ephesians 4:17-24.

"In particular, I want to urge you in the name of the Lord, not to go on living the aimless kind of life that pagans live. Intellectually they are in the dark, and they are estranged from the life of God, without knowledge because they have shut their hearts to it. Their sense of right and wrong once dulled, they have abandoned themselves to sexuality and eagerly pursue a career of indecency of every kind.

"Now this is hardly the way you have learned from Christ, unless you failed to hear him properly when you were taught what the truth is in Jesus. You must give up your old way of life; you must put aside your old self, which gets corrupted by following illusory desires. Your mind must be renewed by a spiritual revolution so that you can put on the new self that has been created in God's way, in the goodness and holiness of the truth."

I can see you smile (*the old self...*) and I hear you protest (*am I a wildly debauched pagan?*). All right, change a few words, but go all the way, go all the way to conversion. There is no denying we live with frivolous thoughts and even more often with negative thoughts. And haven't we unconsciously accepted comfort, that is to say, the most effective way of making a Christian into a pagan? Do we not stubbornly work at making prayer into a kind of intellectual study? And we are not always very honest, we make use of lies, hypocrisy. There are times when we are really mean, lacking in brotherliness, miserly.

And in that kind of a climate, we think we can make beautiful prayer flourish?

— But the purpose of prayer is precisely to get us away from all that!

— Quite right. Providing we really want to. Our prayer is basically bound up with our true determination to reject our old self and with our manifest intention to live like Christ. The rich soil in which prayer thrives (cf. Mt 13:4-24) is profound conversion of heart. There can be honest prayer only when we have decided to pass from the pagan life to life in the Spirit.

There can be no question of delimiting the terrain of our life into a very special area called "the spiritual life" where the old self and the new self confront each other. It is in our *whole life* that we must drive out the old man and follow Christ. That's the reason the term "spiritual life" is quite dangerous if it inclines us to leave all the more concrete aspects of our life outside the domain of the Spirit.

A man who awakens to who he is and awakens to God

I was taking a walk one day in one of the streets of Paris in the company of a "spiritual" man. He pointed out an old building that was being renovated by the addition of a seventh story.

— That's the idea people very often have of the spiritual life: a seventh

47

floor on top of everyday life. A place to lodge the Holy Spirit. No, the Spirit lives in the whole house or not at all. We have only one life, and the whole of it must be transformed by the Spirit.

— How do you visualize this transformation?

— *A man who awakens to who he is and awakens to God.* We must constantly ask these two things of the Spirit. We need to be ever more aware of who we are, of what we are doing, and ever more aware of God's presence. "I am really there, God is really there." We live too far from ourselves and from God, in a climate of escape, boredom, and distraction.

— "Pray constantly. . . ."

— Yes, and that means as fully awake as possible to the Presence. Without the Spirit, life puts us to sleep.

Jesus always showed a great attraction for those who were tireless watchers. He knew that life tends to lull us to sleep. At Gethsemane we feel the full weight of bodies weighed down by sorrow, by things too hard to understand (cf. Mk 14:34-41). During those tragic moments Jesus had only drowsy men around him.

We, too, are often drowsy, heavy with sleep, confused. We struggle to pull ourselves out of this state according to our various temperaments: through action, affective devotions, study, and so on.

We need to go deeper. In a spirit of conversion we need to reach down into our vital center (the "heart" as the Bible uses the word) where we awaken to God. That is where God gives us to ourselves *("if you knew, you would drink from the Wellspring"* (cf. Jn 4:10 ff.). It is from this inner wellspring that we can bring forth activities worthy of men and women.

It is only when we have searched deep within us that we can ask useful questions about how to pray. Let's forget about concocting a "spiritual life" for ourselves. Instead, let us live like men and women who are madly in love with God. This is indeed the grace of all graces.

LET US PLACE OURSELVES IN GOD'S PRESENCE

"Let us place ourselves in God's presence and adore him." How often did I hear these words when I was a young religious! And this was said in a quietly peremptory and habitual way, as if coming into God's presence was altogether normal and natural! Our concern in this meditation is the way to get started in our mental prayer.

Where prayer is concerned, the only thing within our power is to make a good start. After that, God will work within us as he pleases. And unfortunately the motion picture of our distractions will do its worst, as will our nerves or our drowsiness. But when it comes to getting started, we are fully our own masters and hence responsible. Let us consider the evidence of this, which may not be very convincing as yet.

Every time we begin mental prayer we must affirm our determination *to do this and not something else,* and to do it in all honesty. For example, we are not being honest with ourselves when we look at our watch nervously and run to the chapel or elsewhere to jump into our thirty minutes of prayer. Or when we enter into mental prayer mechanically because it's on our schedule. There are some very poor artisans of prayer, and they are the first to claim it serves no purpose.

Mental prayer demands some very calm but intense preliminaries—a ceremonial, if you will. That seems annoying? It used to annoy me. But the day I spoke to a spiritual person about my annoyance, he answered: "Well, do you or don't you want to practice mental prayer?"

A ceremonial of breaking off

The first test of our sincerity is the clean break we make with what we have just been doing. Without such a break we run the risk of merely daydreaming or of getting such a large dose of boredom from our efforts that we will give up mental prayer like so many others.

Everything depends on the peaceable firmness with which we decide to give *these thirty minutes to God.* When this time is integrated into a routine of life, it can help if we repeat to ourselves: *"I freely give this time to the Lord."*

Then the ceremonial of breaking off begins. We need to free ourselves from external and internal turmoil (or perhaps on the contrary shake off our drowsiness), so we can become as attentive to God as is within our power. There are no better methods of achieving this mental relaxation and concentration on God than the old tried and trusted ones. In fact, these methods are coming back into use among young people with the coloration of the East. I refer to such matters as bodily attitudes, slow vocal prayers that are repeated if need be and intensely "lived."

It's a good idea to stand for a few moments, but in a stately attitude, perhaps with arms and hands outstretched in self-offering and expectation. Then a slow genuflection made consciously and solemnly, so that it is really a genuflection of the soul. And finally a very slow sign of the cross, an excellent opportunity to put an end to hasty, bungled signs of the cross.

Beginning mental prayer with a noble use of the body, with these serious and pacifying gestures, dispels our nervousness. When they are made in a very conscious manner they create interior spaces for prayer within us, spaces that are not "dimensions" but a climate. It is a climate of calmness and wide-awakeness in a very special silence of expectation.

If you only knew the gift of God, you would drink from the Wellspring

I also make use of a vocal formula uttered with the same pacifying slowness and the same intense awareness, in order to overcome my tendency to automatism and drowsiness. Each of us must of course choose what seems most effective for him or her. As for me, I say: *"If you only knew the gift of God, you would drink from the Wellspring. The Pasch of your life is at hand."*

This preparation is made with ease or difficulty depending on our temperamental condition that day. But once we have slowly prepared ourselves for our rendezvous with God, we can choose the bodily attitude we shall use during the entire period of prayer. We may want to remain kneeling, or sit down in oriental fashion on the floor. It doesn't really matter what position we choose, providing that it, too, is noble, definite, and expressive. And relaxed! Conducive to good breathing. Let's not confuse prayer with mortification. Our mental vigilance will be mortification enough.

If everything goes well—and at this stage we can act so that everything goes well—we are ready to perform with intensity the capital act of entering into mental prayer. This is *an act of faith in God present to me.*

God is always there

This is the traditional: "Let us place ourselves in God's presence." But to give a better understanding of what these words mean, I suggest four Biblical readings to you.

Holy, Holy, Holy

Isaiah 6:1-8

. . . I saw the Lord Yahweh seated on a high throne; his train filled the sanctuary; above him stood seraphs, ... And they cried out one to another in this way,

"Holy, holy, holy is Yahweh Sabaoth.

His glory fills the whole earth."

The foundations of the threshold shook with the voice of the one who cried out, and the Temple was filled with smoke. I said:

"What a wretched state I am in! I am lost,

for I am a man of unclean lips

and I live among a people of unclean lips,

and my eyes have looked at the King, Yahweh Sabaoth."

Then one of the seraphs flew to me, holding in his hand a live coal which he had taken from the altar with a pair of tongs. With this he touched my mouth and said:

"See now, this has touched your lips,

your sin is taken away,

your iniquity is purged."

Then I heard the voice of the Lord saying:

"Whom shall I send? Who will be my messenger?"

I answered,"Here I am, send me."

The burning bush

Exodus, 3:1-6

. . . Moses came to Horeb, the mountain of God. There the angel of Yahweh appeared to him in the shape of a flame of fire, coming from the middle of a bush.

Moses looked; there was a bush blazing but it was not being burned up. "I must go and look at this strange sight," Moses said. . . .

Now Yahweh saw him go forward to look, and God called to him. . . .

"Moses, Moses! . . .

"Here I am". . . .

"Come no nearer. . . . Take off your shoes, for the place on which you stand is holy ground. I am the God of your Father, . . . the God of Abraham, the God of Isaac, and the God of Jacob." At this Moses covered his face, afraid to look at God.

The Lord's Passage

l Kings 19:8-13

. . . (Elijah) walked for forty days and forty nights until he reached Horeb, the mountain of God. There he went into the cave and spent the night in it. Then the word of Yahweh came to him saying:

"What are you doing here, Elijah?". . .

"I am filled with jealous zeal for Yahweh Sabaoth. . . ."

"Go out and stand on the mountain before Yahweh". . . .

Then Yahweh himself went by. There came a mighty wind, so strong it tore the mountains and shattered the rocks.

But Yahweh was not in the wind.

After the wind came an earthquake. But Yahweh was not in the earthquake.

After the earthquake came a fire. But Yahweh was not in the fire.

And after the fire there came the sound of a gentle breeze. And when Elijah heard this, he covered his face with his cloak. . . .

The prodigal son walks toward his father

Luke 15:17-20

Then he came to his senses and said, "How many of my father's paid servants have more food than they want, and here I am dying of hunger! I will leave this place and go to my father and

53

say: Father I have sinned against heaven and against you; I no longer deserve to be called your son; treat me as one of your paid servants."
So he left the place and went back to his father. While he was still a long way off, his father saw him and was moved with pity. He ran to the boy, clasped him in his arms and kissed him tenderly.

* * * * * * * *

I also find help in the passionate cry of faith of the Psalms: "Yahweh, I do seek your face!" (Ps 27-:9).
I find even greater help in Saint John's verse on God's Presence:
"If anyone loves me he will keep my word,
and my Father will love him,
and we shall come to him
and make our home with him" (Jn 14:23).
I think each of us must search in a very personal way what brings us back into God's presence. We talk about a rendezvous with God, but he is there first, he is always there. In essence, prayer consists in becoming aware of this presence.

It is not necessarily something we feel

No, I must quickly correct this misleading expression "becoming aware." It is a trap. It might lead us to think we must strive mightily to "feel" this presence, or that God will necessarily grant this feeling to us because of the insistence of our mental prayer. We shall come back to the element of "feeling" in mental prayer. For the present let us begin by positioning ourselves very precisely in the domain of faith, that is to say, above and beyond what is felt, seen, and intellectually thought out.

54

Mental prayer is a twofold approach to God in the night: in the night of faith and in the night of love. When we do not *feel* that God loves us, what difference does it make so long as *we know* he loves us? When we don't feel we love God, that is not important. What is important is that we *want* to love him.

From the instant of our capital action of coming into God's presence, let us desire nothing else than to live a moment with God in contemplation and in the union of our wills.

Under God's sun

But first we have to struggle to come into God's presence. I think too many of us rush into a reading, a revision of life, or a point for meditation. We are eager to reflect, to "meditate," but we are meditating far from God! Now, this type of rendezvous with oneself, or with the ideas of a spiritual writer, and even with the "ideas" of the Gospel is certainly not bad, far from it! But that is not mental prayer, that is not a rendezvous of love *directly* with God. It is a common practice to think *about* God and yet remain far from God. But we should not expect this work of reflection to produce the profound transformation that only mental prayer can effectuate. Mental prayer consists in presenting our innermost being to the warmth of God's sun.

There may be days when we will find it terribly hard to place ourselves in God's presence. Let us not hesitate to prolong our effort. If on the contrary we experience a strong attraction to remain quietly under God's sun without doing anything else, we should follow our inclination. In any case, whatever we do during our thirty minutes with God, everything is a means except one act which is the goal of our prayer: the act of remaining determinedly in God's presence so as to let God transform us.

Totally surrendered to your creative action

It has always been hard for me to place myself in God's presence. A piece of advice I received helped me so much that I want to share it with you. We must gropingly construct the vocal formula that is best suited to making us present to ourselves and to God. As an example, here is my formula:

Make me dwell in you.

Peaceful.

Collected.

Wide awake in my faith.

Totally surrendered to your creative action.

In the unconditional love of my brothers and sisters.

This was inspired by the prayer of Sister Elizabeth of the Trinity, the French Carmelite nun, a contemporary of Saint Therese of Lisieux, whose life was totally dedicated to God-Trinity.

The words detach us from everything else and recollect us. They give us the Speaker, sparing us from being imprisoned in a monologue addressed to ourselves or our ideas. They transpose our vital center: "Make me dwell *in you.*"

From that very instant we very often find ourselves in God's presence. (This is a matter of naked faith, of course, it is not something we *feel.*) Then I go on to say the other words very slowly, dwelling on each one and repeating it until it produces its effect.

Peaceful: I await calmness (this word calms me).

Collected: This evokes a mobilization: *I am totally there.* It is even one of life's moments when we most perfectly achieve such a total integration, because dispersion ordinarily causes us much suffering.

Wide awake in my faith: I am becoming increasingly aware that faith is an extraordinary approach to God. *I know it,* and I want to live it by repeating: *wide awake in my faith.*

Totally surrendered to your creative action: These are the most important, the most efficacious words. I offer myself to the power that can transform me. I make an act of faith in a mysterious action that is never lacking when we pray, even though we don't feel anything. I try to be profoundly open to *(I want)* God's will for me. To God's will for me not yet revealed to me, to God's will already indicated by life (my work, my physical state) *and by everything unconditional love for my brothers and sisters demands.*

I find it very difficult, as you surely do, to love without picking and choosing (this person, yes, but that person, never!). At the start of all mental prayer we must make an effort to reject such a sorting out, but instead be firm in our unconditional determination to love. Otherwise, our whole encounter with God in mental prayer is counterfeit.

GOD WILL ACT

To place myself in God's presence means doing everything for my part so that God will bring me into his presence. This act does not merely initiate mental prayer. *It is mental prayer.* We are practicing mental prayer when we remain in this intense certitude of faith that mobilizes our whole being: *God is there and I am there.*

The act of faith, *God is there,* is never strong enough. It is the very act of praying, the act of communion with God. It can take on various aspects. In its most intense form, it is silence. It can also consist in words or gestures. It may be felt or simply lived in naked faith. What matters is that it be a union of being with being, of will with will.

We have a lot of delusions on this matter. We label as prayer actions that are only a preparation for an encounter with God, a reflection about God, or a reflection about our life vis-a-vis God, or perhaps verbal and gesticular expressions of prayer. In such actions there may be an *act of prayer.* But it happens rather frequently that even at those moments we are not trying hard enough to make a contact of faith with God. We are doing something good, but it is not prayer. We are still talking to ourselves, we are not consciously with God, we are not possessed by God's presence.

This is where difficulties with mental prayer begin. Trying to place ourselves in God's presence is something very definite and precise. But what happens afterward?

We are not producers of beautiful thoughts and sentiments

Once we are in God's presence, we must *last*. We must remain there with a loving attention that will make it possible for God to work within us.

To strive to continue our mental prayer means doing everything we can so that God can do something. Where? When? How? We'd like some clarifications on this action of God. But only God can provide that. Mental prayer is the most efficacious school of naked faith, patience, and poverty. We expect everything and we won't see very much. *But we know.* We *believe* that in the measure that our whole being is expectant, receptive, poor, God will do something.

Admittedly, to believe without seeing is not a garment that fits our human shoulders. We reject this austerity, we formulate pleasant notions about mental prayer. We'd like to be producers. We'd like our poor little brains to become intelligent, our hearts, blazing furnaces of love; we'd like our generosity and our courage to be hoisted to the lofty heights of great plans.

The truth is that we remain bone dry, often merely looking forward to the end of the drudgery. *"What am I doing here anyway, fighting off distractions and sleep without producing anything of value?"*

Mental prayer is not something we invent of ourselves and by ourselves

We are not to harbor such ideas! That would lead to disastrous reactions. Either we will allow ourselves to become careless, vague: *It has to be done. So let's do it!* Or else we'll try at all costs to *produce* something. We'll be managing our prayer to the point of forgetting God. Or at least we'll be trying to impose our own law on God.

That will spoil everything. Many well-intentioned persons have abandoned mental prayer because they tried to make of it something they invented of themselves by themselves. I insist so much on this because there are two truths we must never forget: *mental prayer is a very active self-offering, but for the purpose of allowing God to act.*

We don't give God too many opportunities to give us what he really wants to give. Mental prayer is the moment when our whole being, mobilized and receptive, senses its profound poverty but sees it as love's bounty: *"I await everything from you, Lord, I know that you love me."*

Our effort—but it is a great and necessary one—consists in offering to the Lord a being that is very much awake and very hungry. A being who believes against all odds the words of Revelation 3:20:

"I am standing at the door, knocking.

If one of you hears me calling and opens the door,

I will come in to share his meal, side by side with him."

To engage in mental prayer is to organize this intimate rendezvous. But we must let God run the show.

Organizing the tête-à-tête

I have gone into "methods of prayer" to explain them a little to you. There's no use trying to do this, it's too complicated. I've been initiated into a much simpler approach to mental prayer that I shall try to describe.

Let us suppose I have made a rather good start and am in a contact of faith with the Lord. But I feel very dry. I pick up a commentary on the Gospel. I read. Not too much! Problem Number 1 is how not to give in to curiosity and the urge to study.

I am now in God's presence. A sentence from the Gospel or a remark of the commentator soon makes me pause. In my state of expectation and hunger, something has touched me. I allow myself to be filled with it, I "live" before the Lord a new or a renewed conviction. It may arouse faith, or hope, or charity. The essential is that it opens me to God's action. At least, I have faith in God's action, I ask him to act.

This morning, for example, I stayed with Matthew 5:48: *"You must therefore be perfect just as your heavenly Father is perfect."* I "saw" that this does not involve progressing toward something but settling down here and now in a mental climate: I am to love God because I am his son. I held this word "son" on my lips and in my heart. I kept repeating: *"To be your son. To be your son. To have the sentiments of God."*

At this point in mental prayer one often enters into a silence of attention. I am aware that God is working within me, I don't look for anything else. This silence has a quality that does not mislead. When it disintegrates because of distractions (or drowsiness!) I take up the Gospel once more.

Sometimes I am drawn to silence right away. I remain in this silence if I believe it is filled with God's dynamically acting presence. (I prefer to use the word "believe" which belongs to the vocabulary of faith and not the psychologically-oriented word "feel.") There are times when I read, and then I do much more "thinking." It's not easy to describe all of this, and it may not prove useful to you except to show you that the essential element of mental prayer does not consist in what we do but in our flexibility, our patience, and our faith. *"It is God who acts at such a moment."*

The dread of emptiness

When I listen to objections against mental prayer I know there is really only one: it is very hard to endure moments of emptiness. Especially if we don't know whether it is the emptiness of *genuine* or of *spurious* mental prayer. It would be easy to accept an empty moment duly labeled "authentic mental prayer." But we can't help wondering whether this emptiness is loutish or downright slothful.

This is the lament spiritual directors have always heard from those whom they were guiding: *"Am I praying correctly when I endure this emptiness?"*

The experts answer: mental prayer is the most fearsome of all exercises in poverty. At that moment we know nothing and will never know anything about God's work. And therefore we know nothing of the value of our own activity of expectation and receptiveness. Anyone who wants to engage in mental prayer must be prepared for one of the greatest absences of God. This absence is only apparent of course, but it is experienced as an absence! It is a great absence because we can't help imagining that at the very least we'll have a *sense* of his presence. After all, that's why we're there isn't it?

No. God can give this sense of his presence, and he sometimes does. But that isn't the purpose of mental prayer. Our only assurance that we are praying well is when we *have faith* that God is there and is acting, and when we *want* to offer ourselves to his action. To believe and to will are the two arms of the praying person. They are his/her two obstinacies, his/her two gifts to God, *his/her only two sure means of contact with God.*

We came to mental prayer to be led on indiscernible paths, to be fashioned in our innermost depths where sensations and feelings have little importance. But we are so accustomed to live in a climate of sensation and feeling that the radical change is very hard for us. *"I don't feel anything, therefore I'm not doing anything. God isn't doing anything!"* We are in the habit of checking everything out against our reactions, our emotions, our mental images, and our reflection on the data provided by memory or reason. In our mental prayer as in other areas of our life, we would like to feel intelligent and fervent. We're willing to be acted upon by God, but we want to be able to follow the course of his action. In that kind of a situation, we'd really enjoy praying. We would be able to say: *"This morning, I really prayed well!"*

To really pray well is to keep firmly positioned in emptiness. An emptiness that is often very dry, a prayer that is pursued utterly without emotion. It is an exercise in descent into the depths of non-feeling, where resides what is most genuine, most stable, and most perfect in the being of a man or woman: what he/she *is* and what he/she *wants*.

Holding fast to God

I have done a lot of talking about "wanting." It is not a matter of violent tension toward possession or progress. This is the idea we often have of the "will." No, in mental prayer it is a matter of the "love-will," of a very stable and tranquil power of love through which we adhere more or less clearly to something that God is proposing to us. We are then transformed at a vital level of our being. God acts upon our very being through our will which has held fast to his will.

The basic search involved in mental prayer is this contact of wills. Our will conforms (through love) with what God wants for us and through us. And then our life is conformed by our will henceforth to want *the way God wants*. All of this transpires in a sphere of non-feeling that we call emptiness because we are not on the habitual terrain of our consciousness and sensibility.

Your life will judge your mental prayer

— But how about the times this really looks too much like an emptiness born of sloth and failure?

Here's another answer the spiritual masters give: *"Your life will judge your mental prayer."* It is a good sign when we root our mental prayer in a keen, painful conviction of our poverty. It is a good sign, too, when we retain a strong desire for God's action and faith in his action. And also when we maintain great generosity with respect to the demands of fraternal life.

How strange are these minutes of mental prayer, so calm and yet so hard for us! The more God is at work within us, the less we are aware of it and the more dissatisfied we are, but still we are altogether unready to give up. Dissatisfaction and stubbornness are two of the marks of authentic prayer, because we can persevere in mental prayer only when it is an incurable hunger.

BEING WITH GOD ALL DAY?

If our half-hour of mental prayer is simply a moment spent with God in a day without God, it will soon die. It is not genuine mental prayer. One of the criteria for authentic mental prayer is that it permeate the whole of our day with a desire to rejoin God.

This desire must struggle against the very common practice of living a double life: a life with God when we are praying, a life of distraction from God the rest of the time, whether in our work, our recreation, or our encounters.

Why not enjoy God's company right away?

In the beautiful motion picture *The Fiddler on the Roof,* the principal character, the Jew Tevye, chats with God all day. This film gives an intense sense of what a life in the presence of God can be. It reminds us of the simple spirituality of the patriarchs: "I am God, walk before me" (cf. Gn 17:1). Then there was Don Camillo (portrayed in the French movie by Fernandel) who was constantly arguing with Christ.

Perhaps I should cite more compelling examples: Saint Augustine, the man who spoke with God more than any other; Saint Theresa of Avila, who said to Jesus in a very matter-of-fact way: "That man could be one of our friends." What an insight this gives us into the degree of intimacy we humans can attain with the Lord here and now! Since Theresa speaks from experience, why not listen to what she has to say?

"What better company can you find than that of the Master? Picture this Lord to yourself, right by your side. Believe me, do all in your power to make sure this faithful friend is always close to you. If you get into the habit of thinking he is near you, if he sees you are doing this with love and making every effort to please him, then, as the saying goes, you won't be able to get rid of him. He will never be far. He will help you in your labors. Everywhere you go, you will walk in his company. Do you think it is a trifling matter to have such a friend at your side?"

Theresa of Avila spoke these words to those of her nuns who had the greatest trouble meditating. I don't know what effect this text has on you. As for me, every time I reread it a new crack seems to open in the opaque and yet so thin wall that separates us from God while we await the time when we shall see him face-to-face. After all, why wait? Why not enjoy God's company right now? What a challenge to this utterly invisible presence: I don't see you but I won't let go of you. I know you are looking at me.

And here's another insight of Theresa's: "Two people who love one another very much, it would seem, do not even need to use signs to communicate. They have only to look at each other."

God, as the Eastern religions describe him, is abstract and remote! Or else he is close to us but unseeing, "like the sea"! God as we know him has taken on the eyes of a man. To sense that Christ is really looking at us can revolutionize our entire way of life. For that matter, we are very well acquainted with his gaze. There is even a Gospel on Jesus' gaze. It's the Gospel of Mark. We need only call to mind Mark 10:21: *"Jesus looked steadily at him and loved him."* Can anyone reflect for a moment on these words without yearning to be looked at, to be transformed by this gaze?

Above all, we must not force our imagination to lead us to the Jesus who once lived in Palestine. That is not the Jesus who is looking at me now. Christ has risen from the dead, he is living in eternal glory. Christ looks straight at me; he also looks at me through every man, woman, and child I meet: *"What you do to each of them, you do to me"* (cf. Mt 25:40).

This is the simple spirituality of the duets between God and Abraham, God and Moses, God and David, in which we see men attain to an authentic life in common with God. We discover this also in the extraordinary light that Jesus casts on our relations with God in the parable of the prodigal son, when the father says to his elder son: "My son, you are with me always" (Lk 15:31).

And yet this reality is so rarely lived that we should have no illusions about attaining it easily. We must be ready to put up a long, hard fight to achieve a relatively stable awareness of being always with God, to remain under his gaze or steal frequent glances at him.

This battle, as the masters of the spiritual life teach us, can be fought on three fronts. If you find this is demanding and complicated, take only what suits you and invent your own way. The stakes make it worth the effort. We need only think of those many days when we started out by saying we would not let go of God, and found at night that once again we had lived out our whole day without him. But was it really "living"?

Life has two signatories

The first goal of anyone striving to live in God's presence is obviously the intense time of mental prayer. This activity implies a strong determination to resume contact, and it will be granted to us. I've already stressed this in our earlier meditations. But I want to remind you that we must always make a turnabout: we must stop imagining we are calling out to God who is absent. He is always there. We're the ones who are not present to him. He's the one who is waiting for us. This simple experience of reunion is of major importance for the remainder of our day. Indeed, our life in God's presence will never be anything but a series of rapid reunions except for those (perhaps the many?) for whom the points of contact have been transformed into a continuous line.

But is it normal for us to seek contact with God so persistently in our already complicated lives? Yes, because it is not a question of running after a "you and me." That is a kind of privileged escape (or a fear of life!). It is a question of achieving a courageous and effective life to which two signatures have been affixed: *"I did it, God did it."* This is really the most normal way of conceiving our human condition when we remember that at every instant of our life we receive both our being and our action from God himself. Wanting to live in God's presence is not the nostalgic yearning of a Trappist or a Carmelite contemplative. It is, quite frankly, the most realistic way of making the most of a human life.

Needless to say, mental prayer is not our only "concrete" contact with God! We need only think of the intensity with which we sensed his presence the day we were able to forgive, when we succeeded in giving someone a gracious welcome, when we experienced boundless joy, when we successfully completed a noble human task. Every fraternal act is, by its very nature, an authentic return into God's presence. But we are now seeking another kind of "lived" presence, one moreover that cannot fail to inspire us to look lovingly at our brothers and sisters. When we encounter people who are hard, unjust, indifferent, we can bet on it they have not just come from mental prayer. Or else their rendezvous has been with themselves.

Renewing the contact

The second goal of anyone striving to live in God's presence must be to make more intense use of other moments of prayer given us throughout the day. Whenever we can, we need to vigorously renew our contact with God.

This demands more of us than at first appears. Is there anyone who has never said a prayer, heart (and mind!) far from God? What a sorry bungling of our presence to God! We must at all costs progress toward the total rejection of distracted prayer.

I have just made an experiment. I tried never to pray any part of the breviary, even a short one, without engaging in a mini-mental prayer (of three to five minutes). The result has been so amazing that I have been forced to tell myself: "But what was I doing before, anyway?" Surely, I was not resuming an intense contact with God! This also reminds me of a family meal to which a pastor had been invited. He made the sign of the cross, then kept us in silence for some time. This proved very effective in placing us in God's presence.

Without interfering with the total mobilization of our mind on our activities and relations with others, we can find many short moments for reentering God's presence. There are those usually irritating waits for an elevator or a bus. There is that very first instant after we awake in the morning, and the last thought that passes through our mind before we fall asleep.

But right now you may be experiencing a kind of disgust with prayer. You may wonder: Is that living? To use gimmicks to close all the loopholes so as not to let go of God!

I hope my answer will not hurt your feelings. For we are searching for paths together, without shouting to anyone: You're wrong! You're far off-course. I think the stubborn search for a life lived in God's presence is a matter of love. It's a way of loving God which makes us refuse to make a choice between God and living fully immersed in the world. God is not the God of the Carthusians only, but the God of every circumstance. He is the God of the pastor as well as the bus driver. Let anyone who denies we can live a life of love with God, right now and all day long, burn the Bibles. Let him tear out Chapter 16 of the Book of Ezekiel, admittedly addressed to a "people." But who is God if each of us is not a "people" for him?

We are to think about God always?

Now we turn to the third goal, which arouses the greatest reticence and scepticism: Are we to think about God always?

The impression that this is unreasonable and impossible may stem from the fact that we imagine attention to God is of the same nature as attention to our work or to our brothers and sisters. If that were the case, we would have to find a way to constantly pay attention both to God and to earthly matters simultaneously. But God is not numerically one with anything else and he does not exclude anything. He is always there, the wellspring of my life gazing upon my life. He "sees all that is done in secret" (Mt 6:18); he sees me the way no one else can.

This reality we must live with does not compete with other presences, but it modifies them all. In fact, God's presence probably inspires us to be more courageously present to our human tasks, more sensitive and insightful in our presence to our brothers and sisters. And therefore it probably makes us present to our whole life by helping us to put it to the best possible use. Finally, God's presence probably makes our life happy with the happiness of being in love.

I said "probably." I don't know for sure. But I'd like very much to know.

ARE WE TO PRAY OR BUILD UP THE WORLD?

— Mental prayer is a luxury that we can no longer allow ourselves. There is a world to build. Those guys who go in for meditation are not builders.

I know that argument. John Henry, a young religious, never tires of bringing it up.

— Look, think of X... and Y...! You know them, don't you? They wouldn't spoil their meditation for anything in the world. And what sort of guys are they? The're always ready to complain, they are always shirking work, and never ready to say: "Sure, I'm ready to help!" when anyone asks them to perform some service.

We don't leave God when we end our prayer

What answer can I give? It's true. I can't understand how so-and-so, who is so faithful to his rendezvous with mental prayer, can also be so disappointing when one has to work with him. I naively expect from him cordiality, a sense of fair play, and the courage he must have gotten from his contact with God. But there is a wall between his life of prayer and his daily activities. Sometimes I feel like telling him: "You closed your eyes a while ago to seek God's presence. Now open your eyes to seek another presence of God in your job and in your relations with others."

We act as if we were taking leave of God the instant we come away from prayer. But we never leave God! We are talking to him all the time with our words and our actions. He wants to listen to us only in stereo. On the one hand, he records what we say in our prayers. On the other, he records what we say to him with our life. If you are faithful to meditation and take sufficient pains with all your prayers, pay close attention to your relations with God which may be too monophonic. He is expecting *other songs*. He is expecting to hear the song of our relations with our brothers and sisters, the song of our courage, and the song of our justice. And Ah! yes! We are well advised to allow ourselves to be shaken up from time to time by the divine disgust we read about in Amos 5:23-24:

"Let me have no more of the din of your chanting,

no more of your strumming on harps.

But let justice flow like water,

and integrity like an unfailing stream."

Action and contemplation: a very old problem!

Another trend is gaining considerable momentum. It, too, is monophonic! This time, we say to God: "I shall not offer you prayers, but actions. You will judge me on my life. You have told us to build a world. Well, here we go!"

That's the song of my friend John Henry. It is the song of the active life, of the self-sacrificing life. But here, too, some very disturbing examples come to mind. I think of those who don't waste any time praying but who waste time *talking* about building a more just and fraternal world.

Sadly, there are those who never get beyond words, who get drunk on words. Others do get involved in some activity, but without great enthusiasm, and they quickly give it up when obstacles loom.

When I hear them set action in opposition to prayer, I can't help asking the famous question of the *who? Who* is ready, *who* has the strength to build up the world?

74

There is a tendency to search for activities to carry out, without giving sufficient attention to the state of those who are going to involve themselves in them. At this point I hear the protests of my friends in the French Catholic youth workers' movement: *"Action is its own teacher."* Very true, but not action of *any sort.*

Here we see the temptation to a mutilating dualism. We begin by carefully "distinguishing in order to unite"! We say: prayer *and* life; action *and* contemplation; practice mental prayer *and* build up the world.

But by a kind of inevitability that you must have noticed as well as I, the *and* degenerates into an *or:* Practice mental prayer *or* build up the world. And once we are on that course, the *or* impels us to delimit various terrains. *Here,* we are involved in action; there, we are engaged in contemplation.

It's a very old problem! The most recent trend is to make a cocktail out of both: to be at once contemplative and active. Prolonged silent prayer is rediscovered as an antidote to general agitation and to feverish activity that is not really called for.

Without mental prayer, I'm a robot controlled by moods

Through mental prayer I manage my own life (at least a little!). Without mental prayer, my life manages me.

No mental prayer in the morning? I'm going to rush headlong into my day, without an inward glance, never looking back, never taking time to breathe, like a robot who is controlled by moods. What a fine world-builder!

Through mental prayer, on the contrary, I prepare to inhabit my action while maintaining a discreet distance. For I am more than my action. When I identify myself completely with my action, I live that action like a drowning man, a nervous wreck. I don't even think of opening my life to God, to the strength that God is ready to give me. Mental prayer, on the other hand, teaches me the habit of positioning myself inwardly vis-a-vis what I have to do and vis-a-vis God. I am better able to mobilize my energies and I remain ready to entreat God.

Flabby prayer

Actually, there is a way of setting mental prayer in opposition to action that gives mental prayer a very bad image. We end up by thinking it is not an action. Mental prayer is identified with daydreaming, laziness, holy leisure. Whenever I announce to some of my very active friends that I'm going to make my annual retreat, I can expect a gentle understanding smile from them: *"Take a good rest, old boy!"* I grit my teeth and I smile too. How can I explain to them that it's going to be tough work? Perhaps if I explain to them that in zen the sitting position in meditation is a lion's posture!

It is very possible, however, that the image of non-action linked to prayer comes from witnessing too many examples of flabby prayer. That should be a warning. There can be little fruitful dialectic between our daily life and pseudo-mental prayer. Flabby prayer exerts no influence whatever on the remainder of our day. That's what gives the quite legitimate impression that mental prayer is a luxury or a tiresome job that steals time away from building the world. We don't remember to check out the vigor of our prayer from time to time, the inward and outward attitude of the lion ready to attack daily life. The instant we detect a trace of fear of life in our mental prayer's gauge, we are obliged to suspect it of flabbiness.

Should we pray for Lebanon and Central America?

Or perhaps we should suspect our prayer of being too narrow in its horizons. Another poor image of prayer is to see it as individualistic and introverted, head in hands. We have to admit the great outcries for a more just and fraternal world are not worth much more. As a rule, such prayer is without effect on life. Nothing devalues prayer more completely than letting it sink into total non-execution. *"Provide bread to those who don't have any,"* could have been a bugle-call committing us to an effective fraternal life. More often than not, however, it has been a gimmick lost in the joyous hubbub at the start of a meal.

There are times when we are obliged to pray without being able to act, and to pray because we can't act. "God, come to my assistance. Provide some bread. Save the Afghans. Stop the fighting and terrorism in Lebanon. Save Central America."

But that kind of prayer is disastrous when it leaves us untouched. I am not referring here to genuine commitments. Whether they are possible or impossible is a serious but different problem. I am staying with the problem of prayer and its link to what is going on in the world. And I am saying that all prayer should change us, should make us act or prepare us to act. To pray for peace in a particular country should *immediately* make us more of a man or woman of peace right where we are. To say: "Forgive as we forgive" does not always involve immediate forgiveness. But the Christian who has said it a thousand times and who one day fails to forgive—what kind of prayer was he saying?

The person who, after participating in the celebration of the Eucharist and the universal prayer of the Church, picks up all his hatreds and egoisms on the way out is killing within himself the idea that prayer can and must influence his daily life.

All prayer should mobilize us more completely

It is prayers that hover over our heads like inflated balloons without changing anything within us that have made our generation distrust prayer *per se*. Statements like *"All we can do is pray for him,"* or *"Only God can get us out of this mess,"* are regrettable. They appear to juxtapose two worlds, the world in which we can act (and in that case why do we need to pray?) and the world over which we claim (sometimes too hastily) we have no power at all. And then we mobilize God without mobilizing ourselves. That is to twist the meaning of Christian prayer.

All authentically Christian prayer should either mobilize each of us for immediate action or alert us permanently for action. A married couple I know are about to get a divorce. I did what I could, and now I can only mobilize God on their behalf. But my prayer mobilizes me also so I can keep in contact with them and be ready to help them in some way. It also teaches me to be more attentive to the other married couples of my acquaintance.

The reason some of us think prayer tends to demobilize is that we misunderstand its relationship to action. We must take care not to cut prayer off from possible action. At the very least, our prayer must be the reawakening of a strong desire to do something, to be ready for action. When Jesus wants to describe those who please God, the picture he sketches is significant. He doesn't want sleepers, but people who are wide awake. "Belts buckled and searchlights working" (cf. Lk 12:35).

BROAD HORIZONS

Prayer opens wide our doors and windows. God puts us to work on the vast work force of the world. I sensed that the other day as I was reading the opening paragraphs of *Gaudium et Spes* to a group of retreatants:

"The joys and the hopes, the griefs and the anxieties of the men of this age, especially those who are poor or in any way afflicted, these are the joys and hopes, the griefs and anxieties of the followers of Christ. Indeed, nothing genuinely human fails to raise an echo in their hearts. For theirs is a community composed of men. United in Christ, they are led by the Holy Spirit in their journey to the Kingdom of their Father and they have welcomed the news of salvation which is meant for every man. . . . .

"Hence this Second Vatican Council, having probed more profoundly into the mystery of the Church, now addresses itself without hesitation, not only to the sons of the Church and to all who invoke the name of Christ, but to the whole of humanity."*

The whole of humanity. The whole world and its teeming billions become the terrain of my prayer. Not so long ago, when I said,"your Kingdom come," the words didn't spark anything much within me. Now they call forth an image of the whole world. And they call forth many knotty problems, but I love these problems because they snatch me away from petty concerns.

Pastorial Constitution on the Church in the Modern World (Gaudium et Spes), Preface, par. 1 and 2. *(The Sixteen Documents of Vatican II,* Boston, Daughters of St. Paul, 1967, p. 515.

What precisely is the relationship between earthly realities and the Kingdom that is to come?

What is the relationship between what men and women do on this earth and the Kingdom that is to come? Here again, *Gaudium et Spes* is magnificent:

"Through his labors and his native endowments man has ceaselessly striven to better his life. Today, however, especially with the help of science and technology, he has extended his mastery over nearly the whole of nature. . . ." (33,1).

"In the face of these immense efforts which already preoccupy the whole human race, men agitate numerous questions among themselves. What is the meaning and value of this feverish activity? How should all these things be used? To the achievment of what goal are the strivings of individuals and societies heading?" (33,2).

The answer is a brave one:

". . .To believers this point is settled: considered in itself, human activity accords with God's will. For man, created to God's image, received a mandate to subject to himself the earth and all it contains, and to govern the world with justice and holiness. . . ." (34,1).

Wait a minute! When I say *"your Kingdom come,"* that's something else. *Gaudium et Spes* does not hesitate:

"As deformed by sin, the shape of this world will pass away; but we are taught that God is preparing a new dwelling place and a new earth where justice will abide, and whose blessedness will answer and surpass all the longings for peace which spring up in the human heart" (39,1).

But the Council insists on the mysterious bonds that join the earth and eternal life:

". . .the expectation of a new earth must not weaken but rather stimulate our concern for cultivating this one. For here grows the body of a new human family, a body which even now is able to give some kind of foreshadowing of the new age" (39,2).

"Hence, while earthly progress must be carefully distinguished from the growth of Christ's kingdom, to the extent that the former can contribute to the better ordering of human society, it is of vital concern to the Kingdom of God" (39,3).

"...On this earth that Kingdom is already present in mystery. When the Lord returns it will be brought into full flower" (39,3).

In mystery. I look out on broad horizons, but I must accept that the outlines of things to come are not yet clearly defined. The theologians are working at it, the Spirit is pressing us, we are making progress in our thinking about earthly realities. But we must take care not to polarize everything in terms of one aspect alone. Yesterday, we were concerned with "the heavenly." Today, we tend to be concerned with "things of the earth." The correct focus of our search must be the bond between what we are living and what we shall live in the future, the articulation between earthly realities and the Kingdom that is to come.

One thing is certain. We are building a world, but we are not building the Kingdom. Only the power of God can inaugurate the Kingdom. Until the end of time God will remain free in his plans and in his gifts, but he wants us to prepare ourselves intensely and freely for the coming of the Kingdom.

When I pray, asking that the Kingdom come, I think of the end of time when God will be *"all in all"* (1 Cor 15:28). That is the exact definition of the Kingdom.

At the same time I think of the preparation for the Kingdom in the life of cities and nations. These swarms of men and women over the whole earth, the unimaginable agitation of all these lives! How can my prayer contemplate all this and do something about it?

Am I in the wrong religion?

Do Jesus' words make a deep enough impression on me? *"Seek first the Kingdom and its justice, and everything else will be given to you besides"* (cf. Mt 6:33; Lk 12:31).

What does it mean to seek the Kingdom? Who is seeking the Kingdom in our own time?

The wind has changed. Formerly, a question like that would have made us think of someone who goes to church, obeys the moral law heroically, is charitable within his own little universe.

Nowadays, we would more readily think of those who are haunted by injustice in all its forms, by oppression and hatred throughout the world. The fashionable word is *liberation*. Maybe it doesn't appeal too much to me?

To liberate, to give greater freedom. To get enthused over that, we must first take stock of our own emotion or allergy to such words as *"the freedom of the children of God"* (cf. Rm 8:21). Or to Jesus' words: *"So if the Son makes you free, you will be free indeed"* (Jn 8:36). Or to Zechariah's prophecy: *"Blessed be the Lord, . . . for he has visited his people, he has come to their rescue"* (Lk 1:68).

The *Benedictus* is the hymn of liberation. Do I cherish it as a living prayer? Do I make a connection between the powerful yearnings for liberation that rise up from the Third World and salvation in Jesus Christ? Or am I one of those Christians who turn inward in a constricted, timid piety? "Above all, let's not mix religion with politics! And don't put the burden of Nicaragua, Afghanistan, and the Palestinians on our shoulders."

How does it happen that after 2,000 years of Christianity, Jesus who died for all men and to give a great and numberless people to God, has so many disciples imprisoned within narrow horizons? The authors of *Gaudium et Spes* seem to have been painfully aware of these narrow vistas:

"Profound and rapid changes make it more necessary that no one, ignoring the trend of events or drugged by laziness, content himself with a merely individualistic morality" (30,1).

". . . For the more unified the world becomes, the more plainly do the offices of men extend beyond particular groups and spread by degrees to the whole world" (30,2).

All men, the whole world.... May these broad horizons of *Gaudium et Spes* periodically expand our mental prayer to make of it a prayer of contemplation concerning the whole world. The people of God are being born at this very moment at Marseilles, in Santiago, in Moscow, and in Papeete. If I have no interest in that, then I'm in the wrong religion.

"God... has let us know the mystery of his purpose,... that he would bring everything together under Christ, as head, everything in the heavens and everything on earth" (Eph. 1:3,9-10).

Let every man and woman in the entire world prepare for your Kingdom!

When we say: *"Your Kingdom come here and now,"* we are taking a very, very broad view, one that excludes absolutely nobody from salvation. It's not as easy as we would think, being as we are so stubbornly inclined to reject people. When I was a child, I was taught hymns against the Germans. I used to be told to keep away from Protestants as from the plague. Later on I was told to keep away from Freemasons, and then from Communists. A world of encirclements was being built around me: the privileged circle of the baptized and the churchgoers; the circle of the rejected, the divorced, homosexuals. Then, far beyond all that, the circle of the great bizarre religions, and finally the circle of the Godless.

The Godless! I learned to stop putting the *Godlies* on the right and the *Godless* on the left. That is to be the Lord's business at the end of time (cf. Mt 13:49). He certainly does not winnow the way we do.

I have come to see the Church as the sacrament of the Kingdom, the dispenser of the Good News and of the Bread, but not jealously and intractably hoarding them. Rather, I see the Church as a gracious welcome, a mission without barriers. Not too hasty to decree: "You,

83

over here, you possess God. But you, over there, you don't possess God." I see the Church as a sign for everybody, working with everybody. Giving everyone the benefit of the doubt because some day God will be all in all.

Your Kingdom come! These words have been transformed for me into: *Let every man and woman in the world prepare for your Kingdom.*

The Kingdom is being prepared wherever men and women are most truly free

God is for everyone. God acts everywhere. We're the ones who are not present to him, we're the ones who can sneak away. It is therefore less important to inquire where God acts than to see where men and women are made free enough to prepare themselves for the Kingdom.

We have only one example to show us where and how the Kingdom arrives: Jesus. He alone was a man so completely free that he could immerse his whole life into the Father's will. The interplay of freedoms between God and man is the Kingdom that comes or fails to come.

Seen in this light, the whole world is, as it were, one single terrain on which God wants all men and women to become so truly human that they thirst for him and recognize him. The Kingdom *is being prepared* wherever men and women are most truly free. Since the death and resurrection of Christ, which make all things possible, the Kingdom *comes* wherever a man or woman can recognize God well enough to say to him: *"My freedom is to be totally surrendered to You, to live for You."*

I try to imagine this or that person as the sacred place (is anything more sacred?) where God is waiting and perhaps accepts a human person's freedom; a place where, in great secrecy, God and a human person can love one another, where they do indeed love one another. But what do I know about it, anyway?

I also strive to discern in the newspapers (and this is not easy) where freer men and women will be able to recognize one another and thus prepare themselves to recognize God. It seems to me that, starting from these horizons without frontiers, I understand a little better the *modus vivendi* of the committed Christians whether clergy or laity, and the new problems of the Missions.

We are living in a new age. Speaking in general terms, it might be called the age of secularization or of desacralization. There are certain visible signs of change such as the trend for priests and nuns to wear "civilian" garb and the decline in church attendance. Behind these signs there is a continuous slippage toward a life in which nothing is sacred— neither things, nor places, nor persons.

It takes young people by surprise when they are told they may not touch a chalice. As far as they're concerned, it makes no difference whether the Eucharist is celebrated in a church or in any room whatever. No, I take that back. Celebration in a church without preparation by the community doesn't seem to make much sense, it is formalistic. To their mind, a priest is not a man who dresses a certain way or lives a certain kind of life. They ask him: *"When you speak about God, do you really believe what you're saying? When you tell us we must love our brothers and sisters, do you practice what you preach?"* If there is conformity between what he preaches and the way he lives, then, as far as they're concerned, he's a priest. Not because he has been *consecrated* but because he is living a life that consecrates him.

A new kind of prayer for new mentalities

These new ways of looking at things tend to jolt us. As does the discarding of practices that formerly structured our life: the rosary, visits to the Blessed Sacrament, the unabridged breviary.

There are those who cling so tenaciously to the past that they lose their keenness of perception of the present. It is more courageous and more effective, I think, to take a good look at life as it is here and now and to say: *"Let me see, what is happening to prayer? How is it changing?"*

This is not to say that we have to yield in every respect to new trends. Christians are never completely in tune with their times. The Gospel says so clearly: *"The world hates them because they don't belong to the world, just as I don't belong to the world"* (cf. Jn 17:14). But that's the unacceptable aspect of the world. There is another aspect: *"God loved the world so much that he gave his only Son"* (Jn 3:16).

So the Christian must at once love and be on his guard. He must be in tune with the times (that is, with all that God can love about our world) and yet go against the current trends (when something is unacceptable). Obviously, his prayer must go along with the current and yet go against the current. When everything else is changing, why should prayer remain congealed in unrealistic forms? But what should our prayer be like, under the circumstances?

An experimental prayer for our time

Lord, grant that, following the trend of our time,
Nothing may be sacred to me but You,
and every human person, for each of us is an image of You.
Grant that I may always join my search for You
with service to my brothers and sisters.
And so become a person who loves totally.
But grant, too, that going against the current of our time,
I may live poor and wide awake
amid the feast of your gifts.

88

May nothing be sacred to me but You

"You alone are holy!" Life in God's presence, the life of love with God begins when we have a very lofty idea of who God is. At such a moment, I think we delight in restoring a tone of *Sanctus (Holy, holy)* to our prayer: "Who are You, Eternal One?"

In the course of my studies, I had the opportunity to hear a commentary on Isaiah 6:1-8 that profoundly influenced my life. *The glory of the Lord fills the whole earth* (cf. Is 6:3).

Those words are not meant for use only in solemn liturgies. God is God. My life depends on these words. Who is God? Certain self-assured theologians have removed the question-mark. The prayer of our own times reinserts the question-mark through ever more fervent and more stammering adoration.

Let us reflect on how much adoration there is within us. We must go by way of the *Sanctus,* and remain with the *Sanctus.* It is after the vision of God's glory that Isaiah's brief and extraordinary dialogue springs forth, the dialogue that transforms a poor man into God's envoy:

— Whom shall I send? Who will be our messenger?

— Here I am, send me.

What does it matter whether this man wears a sacred uniform, uses sacred objects, and recites ritual prayers? He is being called to have his heart and his lips burned by the glory of God.

Desacralization has swept away superficial formalisms. We no longer have prefabricated adoration; we are becoming apostles without sanctuaries, naked and stammering. But perhaps now we are becoming apostles who are at last the worshippers "in spirit and truth" (Jn 4:23) that the Father wants us to be.

If our prayer is to be the prayer of our own time it must reject the non-lived. We can truthfully say *Sanctus* only when we have become or become once more true worshippers. Does my life reveal that I am a person whom God has captivated and burned?

You have seduced me, Yahweh, ...
I used to say, ...
"I will not speak in his name any more."
Then there seemed to be a fire burning in my heart.

(Jr 20:7-9)

Does a man or woman who has this fire and this sun within need sacred signs? In the present-day desert of the sacred, men and women must come forth for whom God alone is holy.

But every human person is also sacred, an image of You

Desacralization can likewise liberate our eyes so they will better discern the unique value of each and every human person. That is the value that endures, that becomes more visible as the others disappear: *every human person is sacred.*

We would need a parallel meditation on the creation of man in Genesis and on a book concerning the origins of mankind. It is an epic according to the mind of Teilhard de Chardin, in which the pride of God the Creator ("God saw that it was good" Gn 1:10) confronts the tenderness of God the Savior ("God loved the world so much . . . ." Jn 3:16).

Do we have a noble idea of every human person? How could we have sacralized so many things when the sacred resides in every man and woman who can love and be the glory of God? Saint Irenaeus, one of our earliest theologians, used to speak of *"the glory of God living in man."* His words have been repeated countless times. Am I living them?

What do I respect? The other day a pastor was telling me about one of the families in his parish: "That's a really fine family. One of the daughters is a college professor, and they have a son who has made a success of reprocessing metals." I was listening, slightly distracted. I asked myself whether I associated with "fine" people, whether I liked "fine" people.

90

Years of training have made of me, and no doubt of you also, a Christian who is more at home with "fine" people than with those who are down on their luck. But our times can no longer stand for this attraction on the part of clergy and lay Christians for dignitaries and the well-to-do. A little logic is expected of us. We preach that God loves the lowly and the poor, that Jesus pointed to them as signs of salvation: *"The Good News is proclaimed to the poor"* (Mt 11:5). But does anybody like to hobnob with the poor and to share their life?

Let's at least redress the balance. Let's make a table of our relationships. Are we committed to the apostolate 50% or 80%? Do the rich in power, education, and brains make up 50% or 80% of our friends?

Are we *living* in the realistic conviction that every human person is sacred? At this very moment, do we perhaps scorn a certain neurotic woman, a man whose life is a failure, people who are "nobodies." Who are the people that inhabit our prayer? How forcefully do we petition God's help for the humiliated?

I want to become a loving person

How can the Gospel be spread if both clergy and lay Christians are not persons who serve, persons who love? A person is saved when he/she can love the way Christ loved. Whom do we love? We need hardly repeat that the first Christians propagated the Gospel so rapidly because they amazed the pagans: "See how they love one another!" The pagans of our own time have no interest at all in the early Christians. They are watching the Christians of today.

We pray, we participate in the Eucharist. That's very good. And after that? The test of what we really live, the ruthless test of daily life is this: Do prayer and the sacraments really transform us into persons who are ready to help, to serve? Our young people don't go around giving presents. They hate windbags and churchgoers who don't get involved in the struggles and group action around them.

On the other hand, young people have little affection for those who are always milling around but lack wisdom. They want gurus, guides who are truly spiritual. The new trend is very evident. There is an eager search for those who unite adoration with service.

A prayer that is new and adapted to the coming times is one that doesn't hesitate to discuss certain urgent problems with the Lord: *"What can I do today for X. . .?"*

PRAY TO KEEP GOING AGAINST THE CURRENT

We want to become men and women of prayer and compassion. What a captivating program of action! But when we set out to achieve these goals we pile up failure upon failure. We are constantly losing our grasp on God and we act like false brothers and sisters, we are frightful bores and don't do much to help anybody.

I believe very few of us ever reflect on one of the reaons for these failures: a Christian can never belong totally to his own time. In order to respond to the deep yearnings of his age, he must, at least on certain points, go against the current. But if he is in tune with the times (or wants to be), he will not be anxious to examine where and how he can behave differently from others and against his own convictions. It is this unconditional acceptance of the climate of one's times that leads to failure.

A powerful remedy: the eighth beatitude.

"Happy are you when people hate you ... on account of the Son of Man" (Lk 6:22).

"If any man comes to me without hating his father, mother, wife, children, brothers, sisters, yes and his own life too, he cannot be my disciple" (Lk 14:26).

"Father, ... those you have given me ..., the world hated them" (Jn 17:11,14).

I could have gone on at greater length, but the emphasis is clear: *hate* and *be hated*. It is disturbing but true that we can never say: "I shall follow Christ by living the way those around me live."

Unless we become deeply rooted in the conviction that at times we shall have to live a life that goes against the current, we shall be deluding ourselves. We shall imagine we can be men and women of prayer, living by brotherly love, if we live the way almost everybody else is living.

Our environment does not help us to accept the eighth beatitude. Relatives and friends want us to be saints, so long as we don't cause any trouble. They tend to dream more or less consciously of a Christian life that follows the course of the prevailing mentality.

But it's impossible to expect Christian prayer to flourish anywhere and in any circumstance. Present-day life is superficial, fragmented, agitated, and flabby. We judge everything in terms of utility. And in that kind of a life, we think we can practice the twofold spirit of the *Sanctus* and the *Good Samaritan?* We need to realize the incompatibility involved.

Far from the balcony

We are living on a balcony. There, everything makes an impression on us, but we make only furtive, groping contacts based on utility, pleasure, or pain. It is a superficial, fragmented life.

When our prayer seeks only to halt for an instant this continuous influx of things to be lived "on the run," it cuts off nothing. For then our prayer is *of the same breed* as our life: superficial, distracted, fragmented. We pray the way we live. That's hard to change. It's a prayer from the balcony. To put it very brutally, it is non-prayer, during which we have not worshipped or regained a fraternal heart.

For these two actions require us to turn inward to the very center of our being. The first reaction against the current is a stubborn return to the center.

Won't you try to live this meditation right now deep within you? Weren't you reading something in a rather distracted manner? Did you have a sense of being present to yourself and to God? So you say to yourself: "I agree! I'm leaving the balcony." But to go where? To return to the center. What an adventure!

There are methods for doing this. My own personal way has been to add to mental prayer (which is the most intense return to the center) a few minutes of sitting in the zen manner several times a day. Lanza del Vasto recommends the "minute for the call to attention":

"You're in a hurry? Take hold of yourself. You have lots of things to do? Stop, otherwise you'll make some blunders. You have to take care of others? Begin by taking care of yourself or you'll do them harm. For one minute every two hours, stop!"

If you want to live more completely *from within outward* you'll find your own method. The important thing is to refuse to remain on the balcony all the time.

The world blossoms like a flower

We turn away from the balcony to find ourselves. But this image can be misleading. We must not let go of life! We can draw back from the balcony for the wrong reasons. Out of fear of life and to seek refuge in some vague interior cell where we can chat with ourselves and with God. God won't be there. He's never there when we reject life.

It's too bad if the images don't make sense. Leaving the balcony does not mean we enter a closed apartment. It consists in remaining very close to life, eagerly receptive to this life, and withdrawing to the center of our being where we can get a better view of life.

Then, instead of being totally immersed in action, fact-finding sensations, emotions, we can ask ourselves, even as we live: *"How am I living all of this?"*

We must not think we must formulate these questions and lead a life that is constantly turned inward. That would drive us crazy! No. Our return to the center is in itself an insight into what we are doing, into what the others around us are doing.

Turning inward makes us enter into silence. Silence for even one minute already brings so much eqilibrium that we wonder why we use it so little. I am not speaking of a negative silence, a silence in which we stop listening to anything. On the contrary, it is an apprenticeship in the most intense and acute listening: listening to life where it is born.

Everything is being created by God at this very moment. Here and now, (the only place where we humans live), the world is a burgeoning flower. (Or else, alas! the world is spoiled by me and my brothers and sisters.) If I live this experience distractedly, is that living? If, on the contrary, I plunge into the silence of what is coming into being, what a prayer! And what intense love!

Stepping back makes us enter into non-conflict. I don't ask myself any more questions, I'm no longer arguing with myself or with God, or (mentally) with X . . . . I am there, God is there, my brothers and sisters are there. The world is being born to something new. I live these presences, far back from all conflict and worry. I'll return to them very soon, but with a great change of mind and heart.

My vital center

I have stepped back to the place where my personality is constructed minute by minute, where I am constantly being born because that's where I receive and I react. Usually (on the balcony) this twofold movement of reception and reaction—which is the very substance of a human life—goes on almost without me. For example, I have just given this answer when I would have preferred to remain silent or say something different. When I stand back, it is really I who receive and react. Life that was very commonplace becomes intense. I am a responsible creator. I can enter into adoration or quickly see how to be a true brother or sister.

Stepping back actually makes me enter into the realm of person-to-person contacts. At the center of my being I know that I am very mysteriously close to God who is creating me now and wants to carry out a creative action together with me.

At the same time, from my vital center I can at last really look at, listen to, and love my brother and my sister.

And finally here the Spirit is suddenly light and warmth within me.

"I am going to lure her and lead her into the wilderness and speak to her heart" (Ho 1:14).

The Spirit speaks only when we return to the center. That's our desert right in the midst of the rush of modern life, on the front row of our mental circus. If I can reach down to the depths of my heart even for an instant, I experience calm and the Spirit.

A witch's cauldron or a dwelling for God

The modern spiritual writers call it "the center," the Bible has always called it *"the heart."* The innermost depths of our being, the site of our unity, the wellspring of our good and evil reactions.

Jesus is constantly bringing us back to this center. At times he sees it as a witch's cauldron:

"For it is from within, from men's hearts, that evil intentions emerge: fornication, theft, murder, adultery, avarice, malice, deceit, indecency, envy, slander, pride, folly. All these evil things come from within. . . ." (Mk 7:21-23).

And at other times Jesus sees this center as the dwelling where we welcome the Three:

"If anyone loves me . . . we shall come to him and make our home with him" (Jn 14:23; cf. Rv 3:20).

What kind of beings are we, that our center, our heart, can become either the source of abominations, or a dwelling place for God? To step back from the balcony is not simply to withdraw in order to look at life and listen to life. It is to see *the place* from which we are looking. What is this center? Who am I really?

It is madness to allow anything at all to rumble around inside us while we daydream about a prayer of adoration and untiring brotherliness. We must go against the current and let go of the superficial life. We must develop a deep spiritual life even if everyone around us remains on the balcony.

A COMFORTABLE ARMCHAIR, COLD BEER, AND TV

"Ten years from now, there won't be any more Communists or Christians. They'll all be in front of their TV's, glued to their armchairs." I can still hear Brassens say that during an interview.* And one of Bérulle's sayings comes to mind: "We must have the genuine attitude of the poor during mental prayer."

A bizarre association of ideas? Rather, of images. First, I see someone in his armchair, sitting in front of his TV, cold beer within reach. He gets up and goes to another part of the room where, either on his knees, standing, or seated, he seeks to become Bérulle's man of prayer "with the genuine attitude of the poor." Will it work?

I don't say it won't, but we need to check it out. *We belong to our own time,* there's no denying it. That means we are accustomed to comfort and torpor. Or, to speak in concrete terms: a comfortable armchair, cold beer, and TV. And what about mental prayer?

I know that for Bérulle it's a matter of sensing we are poor in spiritual goods. But can we attain to this poverty before God without having lived a life that is poor in material goods? "Happy are the poor in spirit" (cf. Mt 5:3). And we readily think: "I am poor in spirit." Can we be so sure?

---

*Brassens, a famous French folk singer.

God loves these poor because they expect a great deal from him

Let's meditate on that. By a rapid plunge into the Bible. In the beginning we encounter material poverty, the poverty of those who cry out to God because they are *really* hungry. They are miserable, humiliated, they live in agonizing insecurity. God loves these poor, these *anawim*. That's as clear as day. There must be a reason. Whoever grasps this reason will never again be mistaken about poverty. He won't juggle any more with poverty "in spirit."

God loves the poor because they expect a great deal from him. God knew what he was doing when he created man and woman. He wanted them to be extraordinary creatures to whom he would be ready to give beyond measure, and for the sole reason that he loved them. Love gives, love asks. Here we touch the very heart of the matter: what we know about God; what it means to be a human person; what his/her life can be; what his/her prayer must be like.

Father, I need... Father, I beg of you... I realize my total dependence on you. And that's good. I am living in the truth of what I am in relation to you. I am living my radical poverty in the joy of loving you and of expecting everything from you.

But as the centuries roll by, men and women are managing more and more to make a go of things alone. God had foreseen this and it must not displease him. On condition that humans remain humans, defined by *their need for God.* On condition that they be humble, living in a climate of love. The long lineage of the poor of Yahweh culminates in an extraordinary flower of humility: Mary of Nazareth.

In Mary's heart were joined two things that should never be disjoined: material poverty and the spirit of poverty. Mary was one of the little people, the "nobodies." It is from her very simple life that the hymn of Biblical poverty sprang:

My spirit exults in God...

God has looked upon my poverty.

And the Almighty has done great things for me.

... he has routed the proud of heart.
... The hungry he has filled....
The rich he sent empty away.

(Cf. Lk 1:47-53)

What is filling my life?

The interplay of emptiness and fullness implicit in this question indicates that our prayer depends on our way of being poor. It is only when a man or woman is empty of self-confidence that he/she can be filled with trust in God.

When we trust in our own means, in riches of all kinds—money, knowledge, health, luck—-what serious reason do we have for calling upon God? And if our appeals are not serious, then our prayer is simply playacting.

When someone tells me that his/her prayer is "sick," I try to see what is filling his/her life. Our epoch has invented the concept of "filling up." Everybody seems to abhor the slightest emptiness, even for the space of one minute, when we could be really alone vis-a-vis ourselves and vis-a-vis God. Do we ever meet anyone who does not claim to be "frightfully busy"? There's work, commuting, TV, newspapers to read, meetings to attend, shopping, and so on. Lives filled with noise, bustle, and "things." And where does prayer fit into all this? To cry out to God: "I'm hungry!" We have to experience the lack of things we need or want. By dint of emphasizing the little things, we kill our great hungers.

But perhaps you think it's different with us—clergy, nuns, lay apostles, activists.... Perhaps we have been preserved from getting filled up with shoddy goods. But this needs to be confirmed. Even though poor in material goods, no one escapes the pressures of the times. Who can resist the threefold bludgeoning of our own era? Over-information, overwork, and over-consumption. This is translated into wasted time, ineffectual rushing about, and the purchase of things that aren't really necessary. The spirit is always one of being "filled," but filled with what?

As I write this, I examine my own conscience. I don't need to go very far to see that this means I am "loaded down." On my way to work, I have a 45-minute walk or busride. What luck! What a fine bit of emptiness! Suppose I told you the stupid ruminations that fill up this time!

Why is it so hard, dear God, to spend a moment with you? And why is it so hard to drive off negative thoughts and think only of love, only of fraternal projects?

Prayer in the midst of a consumer society

Our present sufficiencies (in the sense that "I have enough to live on and to think about") deaden what is most intense in a prayer that is truly a prayer of the poor. When I recite certain Psalms, I sometimes have this sense of dislocation: These Psalms are too powerful for our petty hungers for God.

We must come back to the Biblical sense of poverty. Spiritual poverty, the emptiness that calls out to God, can be born only from a very real simplicity of life. That's its terrain, the air it breathes. It was in her lowly life that Mary was such a powerful cry to God, such a wholehearted welcome to him.

Material poverty, hunger for God, fraternal accessibility, prayer, these four things are closely interrelated. Before we observe how we pray and how we would like to pray, we need to see how we live and agree to go against the current on this point.

We live in a society where a five-year-old kid may chide his father for having an older, slower car than the neighbors. In such a climate, it is ridiculous to hold to simple and slightly austere tastes. The frantic bids for comfort are misleading. What was a luxury yesterday becomes a "necessity" today. "In our day and age, we can't, after all, be content with...."

It is not enough to give excellent lectures against the current tyranny of money. Everybody knows about that. It is expected that Christians will dare to be anti-money in their way of life. Christians who are free by comparison with those who have money (and are in a position to give some away!). Free by comparison with the ease and security that an impressive checking account can provide.

A fifteen-year-old boy said to me: "My father and mother keep repeating: 'Give us our daily bread', but they don't believe in it." I didn't dare answer this boy. I couldn't help asking myself if I, for one, really believed in it. Or at any rate *how* I believed.

I'm quite aware that my prayer is not at ease amid my human hypocrisies of a man steeped in comfort. I denounce money but I keep flirting with it. It's very hard to live our life as consumers without cheating or worrying about money matters. I have come across Christians who are so obsessed, so hard, and so engrossed with business matters that I can't help wondering: "Where is their God?"

Strong doses of Saint Luke

What's the remedy? Strong doses of Saint Luke. Jesus learned many things by watching Mary live. She was joyously poor, humble, hungry for God, attentive to the needs of others, as we have seen at the marriage feast of Cana. It was Mary who inspired the first beatitude: "Happy are the truly poor!"

As Jesus grew and observed the small world of Nazareth, he saw how money worries and the possession of money encumber and constrict human lives. No one on this earth has been freer than Jesus on this point. The reason Saint Francis of Assisi is so greatly loved is that something of Jesus has been discovered in him.

Jesus, as seen by Luke, is constantly demanding disengagement: "Then, ... they left everything and followed him" (Lk 5:11).

"Alas for you who have your fill now: you shall go hungry" (Lk 6:25).

"As for the (seed) that fell into thorns, this is people who have heard, but as they go on their way they are choked by the worries and riches and pleasures of life. . . ." (Lk 8:14).

"You cannot serve both God and money" (cf. Lk 16:13).

It seems rather gross to us that anyone should imagine we can serve money, serve Mammon. But let's dare take a good look at our lives. We accept, more or less unconsciously, many comforts and conveniences that drive us to compromises with Mammon. And we accept the institutions of a society that serves Mammon.

This twofold acceptance can make us slip into a profoundly antiprayer style of life. Everything has become a matter of buying and selling, calculating. Such things do not fit into God's tastes. We have only to remember Jesus' irritation: "My friend, who appointed me your judge, or the arbitrator of your claims" (Lk 12:14). If I am always counting my money how can I ever enter into prayer? For prayer demands everything, the gift of self and naked trust.

God is awaiting my petitions so he can give me the wherewithal to do *"great things."* We've got to believe it! I know very few people who believe in God's gifts. The idea of giving has been killed by money. Even with God we are always calculating. "Lord, if I do that, perhaps you will. . . ." And yet the Bible keeps telling us we can ask without giving anything in exchange. When God deals with men and women, there is no question of striking a bargain or paying a wage. The less I have the more he will give me, in the measure— *and only in the measure*—of my faith in him. *"Lord, I have nothing, but you love me, and with you I have everything."*

It's hard for us to believe this against all odds unless we have the heart of the poor and unless we live the life of the poor.

WAKE UP!

Life today anesthetizes plans and the courage to carry them out. We are all nervous ants, weary, mentally and spiritually inactive. Life consists of commuting, working, eating and sleeping. And there's the curious system of waiting that puts three-fourths of life on hold. We wait for the workday to end, we wait for the weekend, we wait for our vacation, and we wait for our retirement.

And what am I waiting for? Eternal life? The holiness I dreamt of when I was twenty and that was always put off until tomorrow?

Our times put a strong emphasis on our daily routine. It is there that we act, love, become adults, saints. Providing we don't wait until tomorrow. Tomorrow will be made up of the same minutes, hours, and problems. One of Solzhenitsyn's characters in *Cancer Ward* makes this appeal to intense living through each day's activities: "If you don't know how to make use of the minute, you waste the hour, the day, and life itself."

What does "living" mean?

Everywhere we sense this desire to live more intensely. Novels and motion pictures keep asking: *"What does living mean?"* Or else: *"Give us time to live!"* There is a trend toward improving *the quality of life.* The emphasis is on living more fully, changing our life. We wish we could slow down in order to enjoy *the things of life.*

105

We turn to yoga, zen, the Vittoz method for attention to the bodily, to the mental. We want to look, hear, feel, taste, touch.

The word *contemplation* is popular, together with words like *breathing* and *centering*. But it all remains at the level of words and passing fancies. Actually, most of the people we meet keep themselves frenetically busy in order to escape boredom.

The life of a Christian is not immune to boredom. There's a lot of *talk*, of course! We talk about *"living the faith."* We keep repeating: *"It's better to be than to have."* But we have all slipped into the same slothful feverishness, Christians no less than the others. To calm our anxiety over not living a truly Christian life, we use two great tranquilizers: words and "tomorrow."

If we want to go against the current, we must first become aware of this new aspect of life. We are accepting life as increasingly passive. When someone starts to pray he/she must realize he/she is asleep and must *first of all* wake up, knowing that the purpose of prayer is precisely to keep us awake.

Activity per se does not necessarily make anybody wide awake. At present it is even the strongest kind of opium. What matters is to determine *how* this action is carried on. Action keeps us awake, it intensifies our awareness only if it springs from a life that is inwardly strong enough and attentive enough to create. As a rule, during action we are distracted or asleep. We are merely performers, perhaps merely robots.

This is the crux of the matter: Be awake! I made an experiment during a day of recollection with fifty sisters. The first prayer in common was simply a "performance" devoid of soul. The closing celebration of the Eucharist was a creation. It was the creation of a community which *was* a prayer. There were intensely awake hearts really asking something of God in unison and really thanking God.

Is it possible always to live with such intensity? Surely not. It's already commendable for us to fight bravely against the perpetual danger of slipping into routine performance. This in itself is an important petition for today's Christian: *"Lord, wake me up!"*

Mental prayer keeps time before our eyes

Anyone who practices mental prayer slows his life down and can watch time pass. I am not speaking here of an examen of the past and of resolutions for the future. Such things belong to the realm of meditation, and we should be on our guard against them: they are ways of escaping from the demands of the present. We regret our past failures so strongly and we are so determined to do certain things in the future that we distractedly allow the present to slip through our fingers.

But mental prayer takes hold of the present, it makes the maximum use of the minute to be lived. It is an intense presence to ourselves and to God; it is a piece of our daily life lived in total awareness. There are other moments when we are awake: when we search, when we love, when we serve, when we are artistically creative, when we engage in sports. But mental prayer has a unique intensity because it is our most powerful contact with what is deepest within us, our most impassioned cry to God who wants us to live.

"I have come so that they may have life and have it to the full" (Jn. 10:10).

Mental prayer positions us in an instant, *for the sole purpose of living that instant.* It is the purest and most deeply centered part of our lived experience. For this very reason mental prayer tends to give us, day after day, a wide-awake mode of life. There is so much we can receive and give even in one single day! But only at the price of a continual battle against listlessness and somnolence of spirit.

This is a battle that Jesus demands with an insistence that should give us pause: "Watch yourselves, or your hearts will be coarsened with debauchery and drunkenness and the cares of life.... Stay awake, praying at all times for the strength to survive all that is going to happen, and to stand with confidence before the Son of Man" (Lk 21:34-36).

Obviously, a meditation on the parable of the talents fits in with these thoughts. Every time I reread it for my own reflection or to preach it to others, I get a shock: *"And you, what are you doing with your life? Is this what God is expecting of you?"*

The person who understands neither God nor life

"It is like a man on his way abroad who summoned his servants and entrusted his property to them. To one he gave five talents, to another two, to a third one; each in proportion to his ability. Then he set out.

"The man who had received the five talents promptly went and traded with them and made five more. The man who had received two made two more in the same way. But the man who had received one went off and dug a hole in the ground and hid his master's money" (Mt 25:14-18; cf. 20-30).

In explaining this parable, there is a tendency to emphasize one or another talent that should be developed. The parable has a deeper meaning. The third servant is essentially a man who doesn't understand what God wants of him. *"Who is this God? What is this life that he is entrusting into my hands?"* The man tries clumsily to obey: I won't take any chances, I'll make sure to return intact what he gave me.

By what contrary fate do we, who have Jesus himself to teach us, do the opposite of what he commands? These narrow, anxious lives, this way of treating God as a mean and pitiless judge—that's the way of the third man, the one that Jesus does not want us to be! Jesus expects boldness, initiative on our part that respond to the incredible gift: *"You were born to live, that is unimaginable. If you want to know who God is, think of your own life. God is the great living One*

108

and he gave you the chance to live. Live to the full. Your entire being is the talent. Put it to the very best possible use!"

But you are not to use it in a "self-sufficient" way that would amount to saying: "I have a certain gift and the will to use it. Now, I'll roll up my sleeves and get to work." To make the best possible use of my talents, to live my life to the fullest, means asking God for what I need to live. That is God's total gift. He did not give us a few talents so we could go off and make a success of life by ourselves. God has given us the enormous capacity for a very full life in every sense and with all kinds of talents, providing we are willing to join with him in cultivating the field that is our life.

The awakening, the great awakening, is to believe in the extraordinary gift of life, to dream wild dreams, to see they are unrealizable, and in the end learn who God is: *"With you, is anything impossible?"*

Lord, under your watchful eye and with the energy and courage you want to give me, how can I become a more creative human being?

How can I be more creative?

The first step is obviously to get rid of the delusion of *possessions*. These possessions include not only accumulated material goods but also the gifts we receive but cannot make truly our own through interior acceptance— deep spiritual joy and love.

One evening I was listening to a radio program. A pianist was playing Schumann. My office was quiet and my heart at peace. Suddenly, the music became such an intense joy that I thanked God for being alive. This music became an expression, a fulfillment of my being. I was somehow recreating it the way Schumann had created it. But how many useless possessions I accumulate that will always remain external realities without any creative communication with my deeper self!

And in my relations with others? As a rule, we are simply spectators of the persons we encounter. Here is a man. I know nothing of his interior life. It holds no interest for me; it may even frighten me. But if I reestablish contact with my deeper self, I can contemplate another's life. I receive and I give. I am a creator by my relevant responses, by my sympathy that delights him, by my demands that awaken him.

Seeking also helps us to make our own what we receive through our efforts to comprehend, compare, and perhaps progress. During the French student riots of March and April, 1973, I lived through the first week of the turmoil half-asleep. I kept up with the news reports and commentaries without understanding what it was all about. As a result, I was not able to help one of my students to look at these happenings with the eyes of faith. He reproached me severely for my failure. Once I was awake to the situation I sought materials that could provide food for personal reflection.

But soon afterward, another complicated situation developed. That's the way our life is nowadays, without respite. In order to be creative in our encounters, must we delve into everything? We are crushed under the weight of a great exhaustion. There are too many things to keep track of. And there is neither the time nor the strength to be creative everywhere.

That's certainly true. But let's not give up too quickly. Let's try to be more creative where it is actually possible here and now: in our mental prayer, in our encounters with our brothers and sisters, and in genuine searching. These moments of intense living will influence our whole life and give it a new and vital tone.

The really important thing (and it is often neglected) is to ask God to wake us up. That is the petition of the modern man and woman of prayer.

Lord, grant that I may go against the current of passivity and lassitude, and give me the means to truly live each minute, each hour, each day.

WE ARE ALWAYS REJOICING (?)

People who pray and live sullen lives, what adverse publicity for prayer and for God! We ought to meditate regularly on joy.

On rereading Second Corinthians, I was ashamed: *". . .we are always rejoicing"* (2 Cor 6:10). That whole day I had gone around with a long face. I kept ruminating my worries. *"We are always rejoicing."* What kind of a standard-bearer for the Good News had I been that day? I keep talking about salvation. The reality of salvation in Jesus Christ is peace, freedom, and joy.

As for me, my sun is the Lord!

I know how disappointed people are when, filled with expectations at the thought of meeting a priest, they come upon me at a moment when I am worried, groaning, grumpy. Like a bald barber praising a product to make hair grow, I announce the great joy of Christ. But I arouse scepticism from the start. *"Is that all the effect it has on him?"* If I had entered into the joy of the Gospel, my interior celebration would inspire the world around me to celebrate too. This world that so eagerly awaits *celebration,* one of the key words of our time.

I remember a musical program given by a theatrical group called Crèche (Manger) for the students at the lycée of Neuilly. Nine hundred prep school students, boys and girls, in a crowded auditorium. After the first part of the program which consisted of some twenty songs, I asked a twelve-year-old boy: "Which song did you like best?" Without a second's hesitation he almost shouted: *"Je chante!"* ("I sing!") That was the song the audience had applauded longest and loudest, a folk-psalm by Jean Debruynne and Gaétan de Courrèges.

"Moi, j'ai un soleil plein la tête.
Il rêvait tant de m'inventer
Que je suis né un jour de fête
Avec un gout de liberté.
Pour tenir les chiens de ma peur,
Moi, mon soleil, c'est le Seigneur!
Je ne suis pas un orateur,
Alors, JE CHANTE!"

Translated into English, this song loses much of its charm, but here's the gist of it:

"My head is full of sunshine.
He dreamed so much of inventing me
That I was born on a holiday
With a love of liberty.
To hold back the dogs of my fear,
My sun is the Lord!
I'm no orator,
And so I SING!"

A recording of this song would put you right into the spirit of today's meditation, prepared by using the Psalms and the writings of Saint Paul.

In leafing through the Bible I come across so many texts on joy that I am perplexed. How could so many sad Christians, priests, ministers, and nuns have been born from so much joyousness? When

112

I was very young I had a pal who used to say of a crabby old man: "He's the lumpy mattress that kills you." It wouldn't be a bad idea to take a mirror once in a while, look at ourselves for two minutes and then burst out laughing.

Rejoice, child of God!

Of course, the key text is the good old *Gaudete* from our Sunday Masses of long ago:
"I want you to be happy, always happy in the Lord;
I repeat, what I want is your happiness.
Let your sun
shine before everyone's eyes.
There is no need to worry;
but if there is anything you need, pray for it,
asking God for it with prayer
and thanksgiving.
And that peace of God,
which is so much greater than we can understand,
will guard your hearts and your thoughts,
in Christ Jesus" (cf. Ph 4:4-7).
What strikes us first of all is the word "always." We are obviously being sent to *pray constantly.* Paul joins prayer to joy (cf. 1 Th 5:16). Prayer, joy, and patience go together (cf. Rm 12:11-12). And as he invites us repeatedly to *love always* and to *watch without ceasing,* we have a beautiful picture of a Christian exhibiting five traits: the Christian is joyful in hope, patient in trials, *prays* intensely, is as *wide awake* as possible, and never refuses to *love.*

This beautiful text also brings out the close link between joy and brotherly charity: "Let your sun shine!" We could also translate it by *serenity, indulgence, graciousness.* It is the gentle joy of someone who is living in a climate of love. All of that is sunshine, a reflection of the great sun who is the Lord God.

Bathed in God's sunshine, the believer should radiate a joy that speaks for itself, proclaiming that life on the whole isn't really bad, and that the future looks good.

I have written,"should." Paul knows it is not easy, and he gives us two pieces of advice: *"There is no need to worry;" "If there is anything you need, ask for it."*

There is no need to worry. That advice is as old as the world, and has been given as long as there have been human brains to think with. Jesus saw the whole movie that fills a human head: *"Don't always be worrying like that!"* But when we reread Matthew 6:25-34, we feel like objecting: *"You know, Lord, the birds and the lilies of the fields don't have my bills to pay!"*

But such words are sure to irritate the One who is the Son and who wants us to live like sons: *"Those are the worries of pagans! As for you, you know you have a Father."* In this passage, he hurls the condemnation that rises from the depths of his being whenever he is sick and tired of our bickering: *"You men of little faith!"*

The hallmark of Christian joy consists precisely in that it is bound up with faith. *"You are worried? Plunge deeper into your faith."* In concrete terms: *"Pray, ask!"* That's Paul's second piece of advice in our text: "If there is anything you need, pray for it." And, marvel of serene faith, he adds: *"Ask God for it with prayer and thanks-giving."* (There is the same connection between prayer, joy, and thanks in 1 Thessalonians 5:17-18.) Paul knows that our prayers have *already* been answered more than once and that they are *already* answered as soon as we pray. Christian prayer is imbued with a confidence that nurtures joy. Christian life is unthinkable without this mingling of petitions and thanks in which an imperturbable faith grows. We have a Father in heaven. If we ask him for a fish, he won't give us a serpent (cf. Mt 7:10).

But I'm a long way from this trust of a loving son. I often deserve Jesus' look of discouragement: *"What puny faith!"* I chose to worry and I have lost all joy. I don't know the peace Paul describes and that I envy so much: "The peace of God that exceeds all our efforts, will guard your heart and your thoughts, in Christ Jesus."

In Christ Jesus. The text begins with that *"in"* and ends with the same *"in."* What is joy? It is to remain always with the Lord, *in* the Lord.

Your love makes me dance with joy

Since I have been praying the Psalms in my own tongue, I thought I knew them thoroughly. However, in preparing this meditation, I got a real surprise. I didn't realize they invited us so often to joy. I can't transcribe all the radiant verses. Perhaps you may want to harvest them for yourselves. There is an astonishing vocabulary of joy that I savor more these days when I pick up my breviary: "Sing your joy, exult, dance! My heart rejoices, my soul delights. Your love makes me dance with joy. Happy the people whose God is Yahweh! You are the joy of those who seek you. My God, my joy. Let the whole earth acclaim the Lord, ring, sing, play."

I must stop. But the question I posed a while back is nagging me again. Why is it that so many prayed Psalms (did I say "prayed"?) fail to give us a little extra sunshine to share? "Your love makes me dance with joy." If we were dancing with joy, even inwardly, people would know it.

Lord, if I am not rejoicing, am I dwelling in your love?

The fanfare of joy in Romans 8

I have often given my penitents in the sacrament of reconciliation the eighth chapter of Romans to read as a "penance." Several of them later told me this proved to be a transforming experience for them. Under the impetus of faith, a joy of flags and fanfares bursts forth.

"The reason, therefore, why those who are in Christ Jesus are not condemned, is that the law of the spirit of life in Christ Jesus has set you free..." (Rm 8:1-2).

"The spirit you received is not the spirit of slaves bringing fear into your lives again; it is the spirit of sons..." (Rm 8:14-15).

"I think that what we suffer in this life can never be compared to the glory, as yet unrevealed, which is waiting for us..." (Rm 8:18).

"We know that by turning everything to their good God cooperates with all those who love him..." (Rm 8:28).

"With God on our side who can be against us? Since God did not spare his own Son, but gave him up to benefit us all, we may be certain, after such a gift, that he will not refuse anything he can give..." (Rm 8:31-32).

"Nothing therefore can come between us and the love of Christ, even if we are troubled or worried..." (Rm 8:35).

"These are the trials through which we triumph, by the power of him who loved us" (Rm 8:37).

Surely it was not texts of such power that brought forth the leukemic faith paraded by apostles who go around almost shamefaced and visibly unhappy. A faith that starts out with *"Annuntio vobis gaudium magnum"*—"I bring you news of great joy" (Lk 1:10) is triumphal, simple. There is a God and he loves us, Alleluia!

We were created for happiness

Let us try to understand to what degree joy is one of the hallmarks of the Christian. This is where the three dynamisms of the Christian faith— faith, hope, and love—converge: to know we are loved by God, to realize the meaning of our life is to love him and to love our brothers and sisters joyfully, to look forward to the fullness of eternal joy.

This hope of eternal life changes our present life totally. And here again, why are we almost ashamed of talking about heaven? Let's not allow a few neurotics to terrorize us. Our fantastic joy consists in knowing that the sons and daughters of God cross the frontiers of death. We were created for happiness, for eternal happiness. When all is said and done, anxiety, fear, excruciating pain are simply tunnels leading to joy. We must absolutely read Revelation 21:3-4:

"Here God lives among men. He will make his home among them; they shall be his people, ... He will wipe away all tears from their eyes; there will be no more death, and no more mourning or sadness."

Happiness in all its forms during our present life is but a feeble and partial sign of the greatest joy: we are journeying toward God to share his unending joy. As Saint Paul says in Romans 8:35: Who can tear me away from that?

THE SPIRITUAL REALISM OF THERESE OF LISIEUX

Therese of Lisieux is the saint who showed us how to make the most of our daily life, how to make life holy throughout the week. Perhaps she had been doing some task and had reacted to it in a certain way. She would immediately reflect upon it, then start out in a different way. There has never been a saint who made so much ado about the trifles of life. That's why we can believe her when she tells us over and over, in order to spare us from living in unreality: the Lord can take your life *"as is,"* and do marvelous things with it, but. . . . But? You have to trust him.

When I am weak, I am strong

To trust, to have "faith" in God? That's the classical doctrine! But it doesn't make a dent on us, it never has made a dent on us. Let's try to be possessed by these words of life, the only realistic words.

"Cut off from me, you will bear no spiritual fruit. . . . If you remain in me. . . ask for anything you want. . ." (cf. Jn 15:5-7).

" 'My grace is enough for you: my power is at its best in weakness.' So I shall be very happy to make my weaknesses my special boast, so that the power of Christ may stay over me. . . . For it is when I am weak that I am strong" (2 Cor 12:8-10).

I read: "It is when I am weak that I am strong." But I continue to lament: "There are so many things going wrong—this, and that, and then something else!"

—So it's when you are weak that you can be strong. I have Paul's word for it.

—Paul! Paul! If he were in my shoes!

Therese was more realistic. She lived the very special realism of faith, and took Jesus at his word. Paul and Isaiah are "words of God," as we say. Therese inferred from this: *therefore* they are words to live by.

How can anyone live by these words: *when we are weak, we are strong?* The short years Therese lived in Carmel were haunted by this question. Since I cannot retrace her journey, I shall simply give you an outline of it, without direct quotations. If you like this approach, then you can fill out the outline by reading Therese's own writings and what excellent scholars have written about her.*

Therese's leap toward God

Little by little, a reflex came to govern the whole of Therese's life: *leaping up to God.* For the sake of clarity, I shall divide this movement into three phases. Although they can very well be combined in a single reflex, they can overlap, or even be reversed. I'm sorry to be petrifying what was for Therese a matter of great spontaneity. For the way of life she taught her novices and her correspondents was a flexible, vital reaction, and not some kind of spiritual gimmick.

*The essentials of Therese's "Way" can be found in three pocketsize books:
1. *Manuscrits autobiographiques,* "Livre de vie"
2. *Les mains vides, le message de Therese de Lisieux,* by C. de Meester, "Foi vivante"
3. *Realism spirituel de Therese,* by Victor Sion, "Foi vivante"

The leap in the strict sense

Bad luck comes my way. It may be a health problem, or perhaps X... has done me a dirty trick. It may be an overpowering temptation or a repugnant task to perform. Each of us can add to the list or specify the bad luck.

At such times, Therese tells us, *don't stay there, alone in your corner.* Drop everything *at once,* and leap up to God, leap up into God.

The whole of Therese's life, what has been said and what will ever be said about it—I mean everything!—, can be summed up in this leap upward toward God so as never to live anything alone.

The moment of truth

The immense benefit of leaping up to God is the lucidity, the realism, it brings. When a person is close to God, there can be no question of exaggerating. It is the moment of truth. A little humor is indicated. (Obviously I am not speaking of life's most tragic blows.) We analyze the situation as calmly as possible. If we read the Gospel often enough we come to see, by staying close to Jesus, from what point of view he would examine our problem.

Then we search for two things. How, *in this situation,* I must love. And what is immediately possible *for me.* What the Lord Jesus and life taught Therese is this: first of all to stubbornly return to the obligation to love, God's only commandment.

And in the second place, the need for courage to begin by doing everything that is possible. We soon discover that a great deal is possible to us. Each of us, whoever we may be, has been given an amazing quota of physical and moral strength. Using these energies, and having clearly seen— in God and with God—what is at stake we can very often shoulder the task at hand without waiting, without complaining, without saying "if"—three unrealistic attitudes.

Our leap into God will awaken our courage, and pinpoint the goal of our effort. And above all, it will have the vastly important effect of positioning us once more in God's plan for us: the obligation to love where we are and right now, *in* this particular circumstance. Everything else is fantasy and a wasting of precious life.

This leap into God has hoisted us up to the terrain of great lucidity. Now it will teach us to measure with greater truth than usual our limitations and our weakness. That's "when you are weak, you are strong."

Boundless trust

You have probably followed my thinking up to this point with a tinge of irony. "Those are fine words but they don't go very far in practice. Life is a lot tougher than that. When the really hard blows come your little exercises in lucidity and courage don't make the grade. The very definition of a hard blow is that we can no longer be lucid and courageous. We can only rebel, weep, or sink."

That's true, and that's what Therese learned. She did not lack courage. She proved it when at the age of fifteen she overcame all obstacles and forced her entry into Carmel. She thought she could also go right ahead and take sanctity by frontal assault. But she ran up against the obstacle that cannot be overcome: her wild desires for holiness did not conform to her weakness.

"How can a soul as imperfect as mine aspire to possess the fullness of love? O Jesus, my first, my only Friend, my only Beloved, explain this mystery to me."

That's our mystery, too. We discovered it every time we wanted to do something great and were unable to do it. We were called to love and we failed pitifully. Weak, weak, weak.

Let's try to remember. Did we leap up into God? "Without you, it would be unthinkable, but with you? *With you.*"

That's the double or nothing of holiness. We can fight alone and suffer defeat. Or else we can ask, *really ask,* for the strength to make the impossible step. We must trust God boundlessly, madly. Here the word *madly* says it all.

And then we must fight with whatever weapons are given us. Here again Therese's life is our guarantee. She was not given a softer life, but the means for living a very hard life. Materially speaking, life was hard for her (the bitter cold in Lisieux's unheated monastery!). Then there was the over-regimentation of life; problems of temperamental conflicts that fermented in a cloistered convent. Still another hardship: tuberculosis treated according to the methods of that era. And above and beyond all that, there were the painful temptations against faith. *"When I am weak, I am strong."*

We are loved

Whatever our mode of life, these words have meaning for us. We could be strong if we were willing to be weak. Therese didn't invent anything, but she *lived.* Day after day, she learned that the Lord loves the "little ones," the *"nobodies"* because they are "little ones", "nobodies". Her discovery was to understand that we can live grandly in our littleness, in weakness lived to the limit.

It took me a long time to admit this, although it is the key to the Theresian doctrine. God does not grant us the gift of becoming strong, but gives us the means of living a strong life in our very weakness that draws down his gifts. The "little one" is the one to whom God can give freely. The "big guy" begins by thinking he can jolly well make a go of his life alone. He is sunk. Sunk as far as holiness is concerned. He will make a go of his life, but amid paltry amibitions. He will not have learned to ask for the strength to have boundless desires and to fight the fiercest battles.

But since this seems so simple, why aren't there thousands of Thereses? Why aren't thousands of weak persons snatching from

God just enough love so they can love at the very moment love appears impossible?

The reason, it would seem, is that we have not been well enough schooled to live like beings *who are loved by God.* As long as Therese kept wanting to love, she was treading in place and she kept searching. No, that wasn't the way to go.

The illumination that increasingly lighted her way was the knowledge that she was loved. Then life changed for her. First, we must allow ourselves to be loved, molded. We must learn to receive, to open ourselves to God's creative action. And then we can act in love. *Receiving* is no longer humiliating. (But who invented the notion that receiving from God was humiliating?) And most important of all, we are no longer asked to *believe something that is beyond belief.* The killing frost that aborts many burgeoning saints is this: our inability to believe what God can do with us.

When we follow Therese's life month after month, we can readily discern the stages in her journey toward her trust in love. It was a trust that she tried to describe with the most unconditional adjectives: boundless trust, mad trust, blind trust, reckless trust. Then at the end of her life she spoke only of *love.* If love does not trust madly, why call it love?

But supposing I can't trust as madly as all that?

This is the ultimate objection, the ultimate interior resistance. If I have to trust *that I am loved* with a mad, boundless trust, then it's all over for me. I don't have the necessary degree of conviction.

Here's the answer Therese gives us: Hold fast to life, to realism. We need only live *right now* whatever degree of conviction we have. If our trust is puny, we'll make puny requests. Let's keep trying to make clumsy leaps toward God, let's keep groping for lucid insights and making hesitant requests. But let's get started!

What aborts so many lives intent on being magnificent is that these generous persons dream of advancing with giant steps. Therese teaches us to begin with tiny steps. And to continue in the same way. Little ones always make small steps. But if God's right hand takes hold of them. . . .